IMMIGRANTS IN AMERICA

Chinese Americans

German Americans

Irish Americans

Italian Americans

Japanese Americans

Swedish Americans

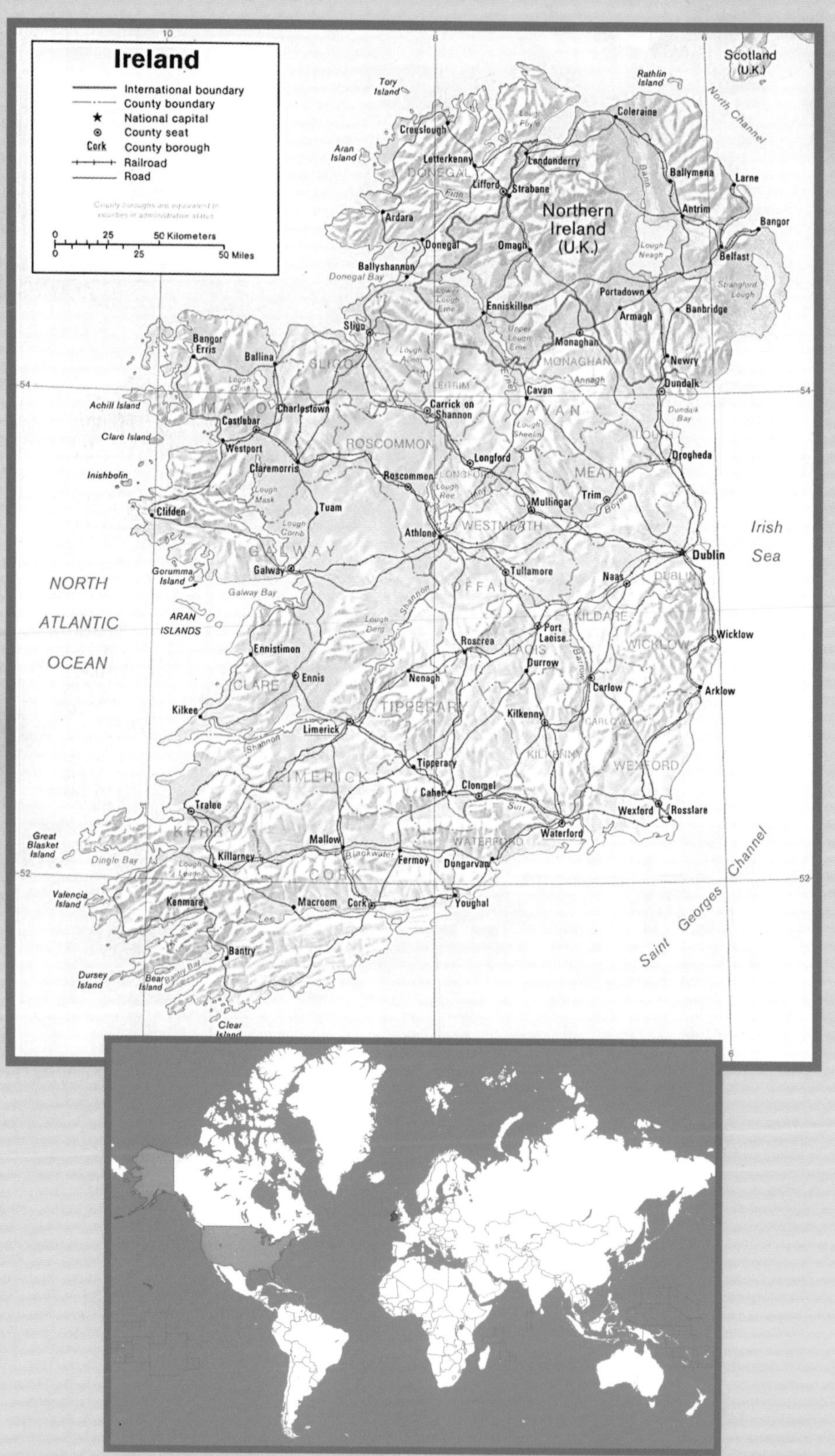
Ireland
International boundary
County boundary
National capital
County seat
Cork County borough
Railroad
Road
0 25 50 Kilometers
0 25 50 Miles
Scotland (U.K.)
Rathlin Island
North Channel
Tory Island
Aran Island
Creeslough
Letterkenny
DONEGAL
Lifford
Strabane
Londonderry
Coleraine
Ballymena
Larne
Antrim
Bangor
Belfast
Northern Ireland (U.K.)
Lough Neagh
Ardara
Donegal
Omagh
Ballyshannon
Donegal Bay
Lower Lough Erne
Enniskillen
Upper Lough Erne
Portadown
Armagh
Banbridge
Strangford Lough
Sligo
SLIGO
Bangor Erris
Ballina
Lough Conn
Lough Allen
LEITRIM
Monaghan
MONAGHAN
Newry
Dundalk
Dundalk Bay
Achill Island
MAYO
Charlestown
Carrick on Shannon
Cavan
CAVAN
Lough Sheelin
Castlebar
Clare Island
Westport
ROSCOMMON
Longford
LONGFORD
Drogheda
LOUTH
MEATH
Inishbolin
Claremorris
Roscommon
Lough Ree
Lough Mask
Trim
Boyne
Mullingar
Clifden
Tuam
Lough Corrib
Athlone
WESTMEATH
GALWAY
Irish Sea
Dublin
DUBLIN
Tullamore
Naas
NORTH ATLANTIC OCEAN
Gorumna Island
Galway
Galway Bay
ARAN ISLANDS
OFFALY
Shannon
Lough Derg
KILDARE
Port Laoise
Wicklow
WICKLOW
Roscrea
LAOIS
Ennistimon
Durrow
Barrow
Ennis
CLARE
Nenagh
Carlow
Arklow
Kilkee
TIPPERARY
Kilkenny
CARLOW
Limerick
KILKENNY
Tipperary
WEXFORD
LIMERICK
Cahir
Clonmel
Suir
Tralee
Wexford
Rosslare
Waterford
KERRY
Great Blasket Island
Mallow
Blackwater
Fermoy
Dungarvan
WATERFORD
Saint Georges Channel
Dingle Bay
Killarney
Lough Leane
CORK
Valencia Island
Kenmare
Macroom
Cork
Youghal
Lee
Bantry
Dursey Island
Bear Island
Bantry Bay
Clear Island
10
8
6
54
52

IMMIGRANTS IN AMERICA

Irish AMERICANS

Kerry A. Graves

Philadelphia

Frontispiece: Map of Ireland with world map inset. Irish immigrants made a long and difficult journey across the Altantic Ocean for a new and better life in America.

CHELSEA HOUSE PUBLISHERS

VP, NEW PRODUCT DEVELOPMENT Sally Cheney
DIRECTOR OF PRODUCTION Kim Shinners
CREATIVE MANAGER Takeshi Takahashi
MANUFACTURING MANAGER Diann Grasse

Staff for IRISH AMERICANS

ASSISTANT EDITOR Kate Sullivan
PRODUCTION EDITOR Jaimie Winkler
PICTURE RESEARCHER Pat Holl
SERIES DESIGNER Takeshi Takahashi
COVER DESIGNER Takeshi Takahashi
LAYOUT 21st Century Publishing and Communications, Inc.

A Haights Cross Communications Company

http://www.chelseahouse.com

First Printing

1 3 5 7 9 8 6 4 2

Library of Congress Cataloging-in-Publication Data

Graves, Kerry A.
Irish Americans / Kerry Graves.
v. cm.—(Immigrants in America)
Contents: The Irish in America—The Emerald Isle—Ships to salvation—Footsteps on a new shore—No Irish need apply—After the famine—Into the melting pot: the Irish-American influence.
Includes bibliographical references and index.
ISBN 0-7910-7128-6HC 0-7910-7511-9PB
1. Irish Americans—History—Juvenile literature. 2. Immigrants—United States—History—Juvenile literature. 3. Ireland—Emigration and immigration—History—Juvenile literature. 4. United States—Emigration and immigration—History—Juvenile literature. [1. Irish Americans. 2. Immigrants.] I. Title. II. Series: Immigrants in America (Chelsea House Publishers)
E184.I6 G715 2002
973'.049162—dc21

2002151394

CONTENTS

INTRODUCTION
A NATION OF NATIONS

Daniel Patrick Moynihan

The Constitution of the United States begins: "We the People of the United States . . ." Yet, as we know, the United States was not then and is not now made up of a single group. It is made up of many peoples. Immigrants and bondsmen from Europe, Asia, the Pacific Islands, Africa, and Central and South America came here or were brought here, and still they come. They forged one nation and made it their own. More than 100 years ago, Walt Whitman expressed this great central fact of America: "Here is not merely a nation, but a teeming Nation of nations."

Although the ingenuity and acts of courage of these immigrants, our ancestors, shaped the North American way of life, we sometimes take their contributions for granted. This fine series, IMMIGRANTS IN AMERICA, examines the experiences and contributions of different immigrant groups and how these contributions determined the future of the United States and Canada.

Immigrants did not abandon their ethnic traditions when they reached the shores of North America. Each ethnic group had its own customs and traditions, and each brought different experiences, accomplishments, skills, values, styles of dress, and tastes in food that lingered long after its arrival. Yet this profusion of differences created a bond among immigrants. Ethnic foods, for example, sometimes became "typically" American, such as frankfurters, pizzas, and tacos.

The United States and Canada are unusual in this respect. Whereas religious and ethnic differences have sparked intolerance throughout the rest of the world, North Americans have struggled to learn how to respect each other's differences and live in harmony.

Our two countries are hardly the only two in which different groups must learn to live together. There is no nation of significant size anywhere in the world that would not be classified as multiethnic. But only in North America are there so *many* different groups, most of them living cheek by jowl with one another.

This is not easy. Look around the world. And it has not always been easy for us. Witness the exclusion of Chinese immigrants, and for practical purposes the Japanese also, in the late nineteenth century. But by the late twentieth century, Chinese and Japanese Americans were the most successful of all the groups recorded by the census. We have had prejudice aplenty, but it has been resisted and recurrently overcome.

The remarkable ability of Americans to live together as one people was seriously threatened by the issue of slavery. Thousands of settlers from the British Isles had arrived in the colonies as indentured servants, agreeing to work for a specified number of years on farms or as apprentices in return for passage to America and room and board. When the first Africans arrived in the then-British colonies during the seventeenth century, some colonists thought that they, too, should be treated as indentured servants. Eventually, the question of whether the Africans should be treated as indentured, like the English, or as slaves who could be owned for life, was considered in a Maryland court. The court's calamitous decree held that blacks were slaves bound to a lifelong servitude, and so also were their children. America went through a time of moral examination and civil war before African slaves and their descendants were finally freed. The principle that all people are created equal had faced its greatest challenge and it survived.

Yet the court ruling that set blacks apart from other races fanned flames of discrimination that burned long after slavery was abolished—and that still flicker today. Indeed, it was about the time of the American Civil War that European theories of evolution were turned to the service of ranking different peoples by their presumed distance from our apelike ancestors!

When the Irish flooded American cities to escape the famine in Ireland, the cartoonists caricatured the typical "Paddy" (a common term for Irish immigrants) as an apelike creature with jutting jaw and sloping forehead.

By the twentieth century, racism and ethnic prejudice had given rise to virulent theories of a Northern European master race. When Adolf Hitler came to power in Germany in 1933, he popularized the notion of an Aryan race. Only a man of the deepest ignorance and evil could have done this. *Aryan* is a Sanskrit word taken from the ancient language of the civilizations that inhabited the Indus Valley, which now includes Pakistan and much of Northern India. The term "Aryan," which means "noble," was first used by the eminent German linguist Max Müller to denote the Indo-European family of languages. Müller was horrified that anyone could think of it in terms of a race of blond-haired, blue-eyed Teutons. But the Nazis embraced the notion of a master race. Anyone with darker and heavier features was considered inferior. Buttressed by these theories, the German Nazi state from 1933 to 1945 set out to destroy European Jews, along with Poles, Gypsies, Russians, and other groups considered inferior. They nearly succeeded. Millions of these people were murdered.

The tragedies brought on by ethnic and racial intolerance throughout the world demonstrate the importance of North America's efforts to create a society free of prejudice and inequality.

A relatively recent example of the New World's desire to resolve ethnic friction nonviolently is the solution that the Canadians found to a conflict between two ethnic groups. A long-standing dispute as to whether Canadian culture was properly English or properly French resurfaced in the mid-1960s, dividing the peoples of the French-speaking Province of Quebec from those of the English-speaking provinces. Relations grew tense, then bitter, then violent. The Royal Commission on Bilingualism and Biculturalism was established to study the growing crisis and to propose measures to ease the tensions. As a result of the commission's recommendations, all official documents and statements from the national government's capital at Ottawa are now issued in both French and English, and bilingual education is encouraged. But the commissioners recorded that there were many other groups as well.

Toward the end of the nineteenth century in the United States, public figures such as Theodore Roosevelt began speaking about "Americanism," deploring "hyphenated Americans" as persons only partly assimilated—later it would be said insufficiently loyal—to their adopted country. Ethnicity was seen by many as a threat to national cohesion, and even to national security. During World War I, referring to German Americans, Roosevelt would speak of "the Hun within." During World War II, immigrant Germans and Italians were classified as "enemy aliens," and Japanese Americans were settled in detention camps. With time, however, we became more accepting as ethnicity emerged as a *form* of Americanism, celebrated in the annual Columbus Day and Steuben Day parades, the West Indian parade, the Pakistani parade, and in New York City the venerable St. Patrick's Day parade, which dates back before the American Revolution.

In time, the Bureau of the Census took note. In 1980, for the first time, the census questionnaire asked, "What is this person's ancestry?" In parentheses, it stated: "For example: Afro-American, English, French, German" and so on through a list of 16 possibilities, followed by "etc." The results were a bit misleading. Remember, it was a new question. Census officials now speculate that because the first European group listed was English, many respondents simply stopped there. The result was an "overcount." By 2000, however, the bureau was getting better.

The 2000 census also asked people to identify their ancestry. More than 80 percent chose one or more groups from a list of 89 different groups. Most people "specified," as the census states, a "single ancestry," but almost a quarter cited "multiple ancestry." So which is it: are we a melting pot or a "Nation of nations"? The answer is both. Americans share a common citizenship, which is the most important fact of our civic life. But most also feel part of one group or another, especially recent arrivals.

Of which there are many indeed! Since 1970 more than 26 million immigrants have entered the United States; most immigrants have entered legally, but of late not all. For the longest time, anyone could enter. Under the Constitution, drawn up in 1797, even the trade in African slaves was protected for 20 years—a hideous practice, but well established in Southern states. In time, however, hostility toward newcomers appeared, notably tinged with racial fears. In 1882 an act of U.S. Congress excluded further Chinese immigration, responding to pressure from Californians anxious about "cheap labor." Next there was agitation to exclude Japanese, which only ended when the Japanese government, in what was termed a "Gentleman's Agreement," consented to withhold passports from Japanese emigrants. Restrictions on Asians continued until 1965.

Indeed, at the end of the nineteenth century there was much talk about the "Anglo-Saxon race" and its many virtues. The United States had reached an informal alliance with Great Britain, and we were setting up an empire of our own that included the Philippines, Cuba, Puerto Rico, and Hawaii. Weren't we different from those "others"? Not exactly. Migration has been going on across the world from the beginning of time and there is no such thing as a pure race. The humorist Finley Peter Dunne wrote: "An Anglo-Saxon…is a German that's forgot who was his parents." Indeed, following the departure of the Romans from Britain in the year A.D. 410, Germanic tribes, including Saxons from northern Germany and Anglos from southern Denmark, migrated into the British Isles. In time they defined what we now call Britain, driving the Celts to Wales and Ireland, with an essentially Celtic Scotland to the north.

Thus immigrants from the British Isles, approximately a third of the present day population of the United States, were already a heterogeneous group. Perhaps even more importantly, they belonged to many different religious denominations including the Puritan, Congregational, Episcopalian, Quaker, and Catholic churches, and even a small community of Sephardic Jews from Brazil! No group made up a majority; religious toleration came about largely because there seemed to be no alternative.

American immigration policy developed in much this way. Though completely open at the beginning, over time, efforts were made to limit the influx of certain immigrant groups, in the manner of the exclusion of Asians in the late nineteenth century and the Southern Europeans by the early twentieth century. By the 1960s, however, America was already too diverse to pretend otherwise, and immigration was opened to all nations.

The people of North America are the descendants of one of the greatest migrations in history. And that migration is not over. Koreans, Vietnamese, Mexicans, Nicaraguans, Pakistanis, Indians, Arabs, and many others are heading for the shores of North America in large numbers. This mix of cultures shapes every aspect of our lives. To understand ourselves, we must know something about our diverse ethnic ancestry. Nothing so defines the North American nations as the motto on the Great Seal of the United States: *E Pluribus Unum*—Out of Many, One. ■

CHAPTER

1 THE IRISH IN AMERICA

THE GREAT POTATO FAMINE

The potato, originally found in Peru's Andes Mountains, was introduced to Ireland in the sixteenth century. It was carried in the holds of trade ships returning from the American colonies. Over the next centuries, millions of poor Irish tenant farmers would become completely dependent on the potato as their only food source. When a fungus struck the potato fields in 1845, it was the first of six years of partial or complete crop failures. The extreme poverty, starvation, and ensuing epidemic illnesses suffered by Ireland's farm laborers because of this blight continued until 1855. This decade of hardship and death is collectively called the "Potato Famine." One million Irish died during the Famine, and another million were forced to immigrate to foreign countries to avoid death. Ironically, most of these immigrants crossed the

Soon after the potato was introduced to Ireland from Peru in the sixteenth century, Irish farmers quickly became dependent upon it as a staple food source. When a fungus ravaged Irish potato crops in 1845, the resulting starvation and disease caused a million deaths.

ocean to America in the cargo holds of trade ships similar to those that had first brought the potato to their nation's shores.

EARLY IMMIGRANTS

The Famine immigrants were not the first group of Irish men and women to travel to the United States. In fact, many different groups had sought a better life in America, centuries before the Famine. The earliest immigrants were congregations of Protestants from Northern Ireland seeking religious freedom in the late 1600s. They continued to arrive up until the American Revolution in 1776. In addition, laborers from the lower socioeconomic classes who could not afford ship passage fees came to the colonies as indentured servants who signed a contract to work for someone for a specified number of years to pay back the cost of their passage.

After the American Revolution, small farmers, artisans, businessmen, and professionals from Northern Ireland continued to settle in America. By the 1840s, most Irish immigrants in the United States were relatively wealthy, usually Protestant, workingmen and women, who had left Ireland because of what they believed was an unfair system of taxation imposed under

Irish Immigration in Numbers

Irish Immigration to the United States, 1821–2000. Courtesy of the United States Immigration and Naturalization Service.

Decade	Number of Immigrants
1821–1830	50,724
1831–1840	207,381
1841–1850	780,719
1851–1860	914,119
1861–1870	435,778
1871–1880	436,871
1881–1890	655,482
1891–1900	388,416
1901–1910	339,065
1911–1920	146,181
1921–1930	211,234
1931–1940	10,973
1941–1950	19,789
1951–1960	48,362
1961–1970	32,966
1971–1980	11,490
1981–1990	31,969
1991–2000	56,950
TOTAL	4,782,083

British rule, and also because of the religious intolerance they felt from the Anglican Church. After the 1820s, more and more Catholics from southern Ireland arrived. A population explosion had forced them to choose emigration because there was no land available for them to farm. By the 1840s, roughly one million Irish immigrants had left their homes in Ireland.

The farm laborers of Catholic Ireland had been subjects of British rule for centuries when the blight infected their potato crop in 1845. They had very little in common with the ruling classes who owned the land they worked on. Harsh penal codes prohibiting Catholics from owning property, receiving an education, speaking their native Gaelic language, and publicly practicing their Catholic faith were some of the most restrictive laws the Irish families had to endure. They paid the rent on the land they farmed by selling off crops. When the potato crop failed, many who were unable to afford their rents and taxes were forced off the land, and their homes were destroyed by the landlords.

The British ruling class could not or would not provide enough relief to save Ireland's poor. Facing starvation, no job prospects, and certain illness as they roamed the Irish countryside, many felt there were no options left for them in Ireland. More than 5,000 ships brought immigrants to North America during the Famine.

Although more than one million people fled Ireland during the Potato Famine, this was not the largest group of Irish to settle in America. Between 1855 and 1921, when Ireland became independent of Great Britain, additional thousands were driven to emigrate because of crop failures and the accompanying collapse of the farm economy. By 1890, there were 4.8 million first- and second-generation Irish in America and just under 5 million in 1900. This exceeded the total population of Ireland by a half-million.

LOST CHILDREN IMMIGRANTS

Although most Famine-era immigrants coming to America traveled as family groups, immigrants coming in the 1850s and 1860s were often individuals seeking a better life. The immigrants

The Potato Famine, along with the collapse of the farm economy following Ireland's independence from Britain, resulted in waves of Irish emigration. Entire families left their farms and sailed for America. By 1900, there were more Irish in America than in Ireland! This drawing shows a priest blessing an Irish family as they prepare to leave Ireland in search of a better life.

had a sibling, child, or even a parent who was established in America and who sent money home to Ireland to finance their emigration. Annie Moore, the first immigrant through Ellis Island, came to America after her parents and found them on her arrival. She and her brother were luckier than many. Accounts of family members who could not find one another were common. If parents did not receive word from Ireland about what ship their children were traveling on, they had no idea on what date they would arrive. Some children were so young that, when asked their parents' names, they could reply only "Mother and Father." Newspapers carried advertisements from parents searching for lost children, and groups of these passage orphans roamed the waterfront areas where their ships had left them.

Tracing Your Roots

If you are interested in discovering your Irish roots, there are a variety of resources to help you in your research. Begin in the present and work into the past, taking accurate and organized notes. Although the names of your ancestors are the most important record on the family tree you will create, it is necessary to add details to distinguish your family members from others.

Detailed records are organized by family groups, sets of parents, and their children. This includes birth, marriage, and death dates and their locations for each person. It is possible to print blank charts from genealogy research websites, or you can use free online or downloadable genealogy record programs instead.

Start from your memory, listing yourself, your parents, and your siblings on your blank family group record. Many records such as census, land titles, and birth, marriage, and death certificates list information by county as well as city. Always include county information as you compile your records. Then begin a new family group record for each of your parents, listing their siblings and their parents. Once you have listed as much information as you can remember, ask your relatives to fill in any blanks. It is easiest to work on one family line at a time, such as your maternal grandfather's family.

Your living relatives are a valuable source of information. Their memories and stories are a meaningful part of your family tree. They also will have a great deal of information recorded in family bibles, diaries, letters, photographs, birth certificates, marriage licenses, deeds, wills, and obituary clippings. As you fill in your record, list whether the source of information was a letter, a conversation with your grandmother, or information from your great-uncle's military discharge papers that were stored in the attic. This will make it easier to verify your information.

Local history centers and genealogy societies specialize in assisting people in compiling records and have searchable data such as microfilm census records. Your local library also has many resources. The Internet has made it easy to research your family from home, and there are hundreds of websites for genealogists to access particular information. Many sites allow researchers documenting the same family lines to share their files with each other. It is always important to double-check the sources others used to find their information so that you can be sure that your ancestors are truly the same.

SEEKING A BETTER LIFE

Whatever their religious or socioeconomic background, Irish immigrants all sought the promise of a better life in America. Letters from earlier immigrants had told of the many job prospects for anyone who could brave the harrowing four- to six-week trip across the Atlantic Ocean. Irish immigrants predominantly settled along the eastern seaboard where their ships arrived. Hundreds of thousands formed slum communities in cities such as New York, Philadelphia, Boston, Baltimore, and New Orleans. Jobs on canals and railroad construction brought Irish immigrants to the Midwest, where they helped build Chicago, St. Paul, and Milwaukee. The West was home to Irish miners and rail workers, and Irish men formed a large part of the population in the early history of cities such as San Francisco, Butte, and Denver. By the end of the nineteenth century, Irish men and women could be found in all regions of the country.

Although the Famine Irish formed less than one-third of all immigrants to the United States during the 1800s, they are a notable group. Some historians have described them as the original "huddled masses" who streamed into America. Indeed, they were the first group to arrive by the hundreds of thousands, creating a distinct community within the American culture. They faced discrimination, fought off poverty, and withstood horrible living conditions as they bore the brunt of American anti-foreign and anti-Catholic attitudes.

FINDING ACCEPTANCE

The experiences of the Irish in America made them band together and work as a group to find success in politics, industry, and entertainment. A measure of their successful assimilation into American culture today is the fact that they are not viewed as a separate ethnic group any longer. There are no longer exclusively Irish neighborhoods in the cities across the nation, although more than 38 million Americans claim Irish ancestry. The recent interest in Irish literature, music, and dance in the

Possibly the most widely recognized feature of Irish culture in America is the St. Patrick's Day Parade. But the Irish also contributed a rich tradition of music, dance, and literature to American culture.

United States points to the acceptance of Irish roots as a vital part of American culture. At least on St. Patrick's Day each year, everyone is a little bit Irish, as we all celebrate the accomplishments of the Irish in America.

CHAPTER

2

THE EMERALD ISLE

PHYSICAL FEATURES

The Emerald Isle is another name for Ireland. It is an apt description of Ireland's low and rolling interior plain, which is always lush and green from abundant rainfall in Ireland's temperate climate. Th Republic of Ireland, which takes up 80 percent of the island of Ireland, is only 27,136 square miles (70,280 square kilometers) in area, about the same size as West Virginia. Located in Western Europe, the Irish Sea and St. George's Channel separate this island jewel from the west and southwest coasts of Great Britain, which lies between 11 and 120 miles (18 to 193 kilometers) away. The Atlantic Ocean surrounds the remainder of the island, from the northern region of Ulster southward. The western coast's sea cliffs give way to rocky southern shores where the Atlantic Ocean meets the Celtic Sea.

Ireland has been nicknamed the Emerald Isle for her rolling green hills, owing to its temperate climate and ample rainfall.

EARLY INHABITANTS

The earliest recorded inhabitants of Ireland, the Gaelic-speaking Celts (Kelts) often raided Britain. Early in the fifth century, one such group of marauding Celts returned with a teenage slave named Patrick, who by introducing his captors to Christianity, would go on to become Ireland's patron saint—

St. Patrick. Catholicism spread throughout Ireland during the Middle Ages (A.D. 500–1500), and monks traveled abroad as missionaries. Other groups of Irish ventured to Europe as traders, on religious pilgrimages, and as students.

The Vikings' arrival across the North Atlantic in 795 led to a 200-year occupation of the eastern portion of Ireland. Many forts grew into today's towns and cities, including the modern capital of Dublin. The Celtic king Brian Boru formed an army that defeated the Vikings in 1014, driving them from Ireland's shore.

The victory and Irish control did not last even 150 years. The Normans, who had taken control of England in 1066, assumed control over Ireland in 1155 and invaded by crossing the Irish Sea in 1169. The Norman king, Henry II, began the long history of English occupation of Irish land by granting holdings in eastern Ireland to Norman lords. Norman control continued into the 1600s.

CHANGE IN RELIGION

Throughout this period, both Celtic and Norman families practiced Catholicism. This changed in 1534, when England's King Henry VIII broke away from the Catholic Church to form the Church of England. After declaring himself king of Ireland in 1541, he and his daughter, Elizabeth I, tried to force the Irish to accept Protestantism. They felt a shared religion would make their control of Ireland easier and therefore they favored Protestants with land and political power. Elizabeth's successor, James I, went one step further. Although his wife was Catholic, in order to keep control of the monarchy, James cultivated the support of Scottish Presbyterians by granting them lands in Ulster in 1609. This region of Northern Ireland, cut off from Catholic Ireland (The Republic of Ireland), is part of Great Britain today. Local Protestant landlords passed laws to increase their control of Irish land, and Catholics were forbidden to attend school or be hired for jobs in this Ulster region.

Although the Irish had driven the Vikings from their shores in 1014, their independence was short-lived. In 1169, the Normans, who had taken control of England, now invaded Ireland. The Norman king, Henry II, quickly granted holdings in eastern Ireland to Norman lords.

Rebellion in England in 1649 established Oliver Cromwell as lord protector of England. As a Protestant, Cromwell felt it his duty to obliterate (remove) Catholicism in Ireland, since Irish rebellions had resulted in many casualties of British soldiers and landholders. Once again, invading across the Irish Sea, troops killed men, women, and children indiscriminately. Churches were burned and priests punished by death. To be Catholic was treasonous, and several thousand Irish men and women were sent across the ocean to British colonies in the Americas to be slaves as their punishment. Cromwell granted vast portions of farmland throughout Ireland to his supporters, who became landlords to the Irish farm families. Most of these "absentee" landlords continued to live in England, with their only ties to Ireland shown in account books through the rents and taxes they collected.

DEFEAT OF THE CATHOLICS

Catholicism returned to the throne of England in 1669 when the Stuart family was restored to the monarchy. However, the English people were strongly Protestant, and by 1688 rule was granted to the Protestant William of Orange of the Netherlands. His deposed father-in-law, King James II, fled to Ireland, where his Catholic supporters defended him against William's invading troops. The Catholics were defeated in 1690, resulting in the identification of Protestant Irish as "Orangemen."

BRITISH RESTRICTIONS ON CATHOLICS

Life became restrictive for Catholics who remained in Ireland—roughly 80 percent of the island's population. Britain's Parliament passed strict "penal laws" between the 1690s and 1715 which deprived Catholics of numerous civil rights, including the right to vote, hold government and other professional jobs, attend school, attend Catholic Mass, and own land. Violations of these codes were punishable by fines, public whippings, imprisonment, or death. These harsh limitations led to the immigration of thousands of Irish men and women to continental Europe. Some left for the American colonies as indentured servants, promising to work four to seven years for whomever would pay their passage.

The British did not limit their restrictions to Catholics alone. In the north, the Presbyterian Ulster Scots were burdened with heavy import taxes on cloth shipped to English markets. During the 1700s, many waves of these Scotch-Irish immigrated to colonies in New England, Virginia, the Carolinas, and farther south in search of economic freedom. These families were relatively wealthy and could afford to bring their entire households and weaving businesses to establish a new life in a new land.

IRELAND TURNS TO FARMING

To the south, Irish Catholics were feeling the pinch of British control. The Act of Union passed by England in 1801 had officially joined Ireland with England, Scotland, and Wales to form the United Kingdom, further dividing the two religious groups. Economic development in Ireland was directed by the needs of the British market. Rather than develop Irish industries, England imported raw materials from Ireland for use in its own production of goods. With native industries failing, most Irish, who were blocked from holding professional jobs, could only turn to farming and the export of food to meet economic demands. In 1841, roughly 90 to 95 percent of Ireland's population lived in rural farm areas.

A farming hierarchy had developed among Irish farmers under the control of British absentee landlords. Families who had owned their own farms before the penal laws could now only rent the same fields. Over generations, as families grew, these farmers subdivided their land through "partible" inheritance. That is, each son received an equal portion of the family's farmland on the death of his father. Daughters received an equal portion of land as well as a dowry for marriage. Of course, these inheritances were not for legal ownership of the property, but for the right of tenancy on the land. Over time, rents and taxes inevitably increased, and only the smaller farm holdings were remotely affordable for most Irish families. Even so, 75 percent of farms were 20 acres or less, and of those, half were smaller than 10 acres.

Among these farmers were poorer groups of Irish families who also depended on farming for their survival. One group, called "cottiers," essentially subleased patches of land from the tenant farmers. They would rent a garden patch and a cottage from the farmers, often no more than two or three acres in total. They paid rent on their property through labor on the farmer's land or by a combination of labor and cash. By the 1830s, over half the farmers' income went to paying rent on their land. Below this group was the landless "conacre" tenant class. These families had no land of their own, but were given access to small garden plots to raise food. They did not have any form of lodging as part of their contracts and often squatted illegally on the farms where they were hired as day laborers. These cottiers and conacre farmers outnumbered the tenant farmers by a margin of four to one.

RURAL LIFE

Rural families were isolated from one another by the sprawling design of Irish farms and settlements. Unlike communities in the rest of Europe, where town squares and roads organized a commercial center with farmland in the surrounding countryside, there were no shops or streets in Irish farm communities. Clusters of rough cottages housed extended families of up to a dozen people, who often shared space with a pig or cow. In 1841, 40 percent of these cottages were made up of one room, with nearly another 40 percent having two to four rooms. The average size of an Irish cottage was only 250 square feet. Building materials came from whatever could be taken from the land around them. Rock or muddy peat walls were topped by grass-thatched roofs over a packed dirt floor. As families grew and children married, additional cottages were built nearby. Relatives shared with one another and with their neighbors, producing nearly everything they used. Local government officials did not exist in communities such as these, and the advice of the local priest and church teachings provided the only laws by which rural Irish men and women led their lives.

To pay the ever-increasing rents, families had to grow more lucrative crops such as oats, wheat, or barley to raise pigs, sheep, and cattle for slaughter. Every cent went toward rent and taxes, and only the smallest plots of land could be spared for raising food for the family. The potato was the salvation of Irish farm families. It required no tools for planting or harvesting other than a shovel. Large numbers of potatoes could be grown in a small plot of land and could be stored for many months in underground pits covered with straw. Best of all, the potato was nourishing and easy to prepare, and thousands of Irish families consumed only boiled potatoes cooked over a fire for almost all of their meals.

Frequently, rents could not be covered by the sale of crops. Men often left their wives and children during the "hungry months" of July and August and traveled to England in search of work. Usually, by that time in the year, the stored potatoes from the previous year had run out, and the new crop was not yet ready for harvest. During the winter months, women and children would weave linen cloth from the long fibers of the flax plant or would make lace to sell in British or European markets, while their families did without and dressed in rags. In the evenings, when it became too dark to work, families would gather together to tell stories of Ireland's history, reciting poems in Gaelic, which had been passed down for generations. These poems recalled the days of Celtic kings. Songs of armed rebellion and uprisings against British rule celebrated fierce Irish pride, often accompanied by the strains of a fiddle. Recalling their heritage often kept many Irish from despair while poverty led them further and further into debt.

HARDSHIPS LEAD TO EMIGRATION

Finding employment became increasingly difficult as the Irish population tripled between 1740 and 1840 from four million to more than eight million people. Most of these people were landless and semi-landless farmers who lived in rural cottages. Even by 1851, there were only 14 towns in Ireland that held 10,000 people or more. In these cities, unemployment was high and slums abounded, so urban life was often no better than that of the poverty-stricken farmers.

Destitute men who could not cope often turned to alcohol, whereas their families turned to begging for food to survive. Others vented their frustrations by rioting against their British landlords. Failed rebellions in 1798 and 1803 sent political refugees to the newly formed United States. Others immigrated later in the 1820s and 1830s to such English cities as London, Liverpool, or Manchester. Still other prospective émigrés answered American advertisements that appeared in Dublin and Belfast for jobs building canals to connect the Atlantic seaboard with the Great Lakes region. Weavers, spinners, and other craftsmen were being forced out of work because of technological advancements in England.

As England became more industrialized, Ireland's manufactured products could not compete with the mass-produced goods on the English market. Many of these Irish craftsmen, having some financial resources, bought passage to the United States for their families to pursue their trades abroad. By 1840, more than one million Irish had emigrated from their homes.

The British landlords were not sorry to see the Irish leave. Tenant taxes that could not be paid were passed on to the landlords for payment. Many Irish estates were already

Unable to pay tenant taxes to their British landlords, Irish families found themselves evicted from their small homesteads. This photo shows one such Irish family who found themselves homeless.

heavily in debt, and the only way to increase profitability was to convert the small tenant holdings to larger fields for grain crops or for pasturing livestock. The only way to do this was by first evicting tenant families who were unable to pay rents, many of whom had debts stretching back for generations.

POTATO BLIGHT

The Dublin *Freeman's Journal* in 1845 reported that a mysterious fungus had taken hold in the potato fields of Ireland. The blight was described as destroying acre upon acre of potatoes overnight. "In one instance the [farmer] had been digging potatoes—the finest he had ever seen—from a particular field . . . up to Monday last; and on digging in the same ridge on Tuesday he found the tubers blasted, and unfit for the use of man or beast." The fungus, later named *Phytophthora infestans*, carried across the country by winds, struck at the exposed leaves of the the plants first, withering the stalks and turning the leaves

Famine Song

The town of Skibbereen is located near the extreme southwestern point of Ireland. During the Potato Famine, the southern and western counties were hardest hit by the crop failure. The first recorded death caused by the Famine occurred in Skibbereen, and soon the town and surrounding areas were filled with the corpses of the dead and suffering. Yet, in spite of their immense suffering and loss, the Skibbereen émigrés would hold fond memories of their homeland, as evidenced by the text of the song that follows. The song reflects the Skibbereen natives' great pride in Ireland, and the residual anger they felt toward the British. As the final stanza proves, even subsequent generations of men and women born or raised in America were fiercely proud of their Irish heritage.

SKIBBEREEN

Oh, father dear, I often hear you speak of Erin's Isle,
Her lofty scenes and valleys green, her mountains rude and wild.
They say it is a lovely land wherein a prince might dwell,
Oh why did you abandon it? The reason to me tell.

a dry, crumbly brown. Farmers rushed to save as much of the crop as they could. However, rainfall pushed the fungus spores through the soil down to the potatoes as well, and in storage, they turned into a black and mushy mass, giving off a putrid stench. This smell became familiar across Ireland, since half of the 1845 crop was consumed by the blight. Once in the soil, the fungus was difficult to eradicate. The crop of 1846 nearly failed completely.

BRITISH FORCE EXPORT OF FOOD

Although shiploads of relief supplies were sent to Ireland from the United States and Europe, the process to widely distribute

Oh, son I loved my native land with energy and pride,
Till a blight came o'er my crops—my sheep, my cattle died.
My rent and taxes were too high, I could not them redeem,
And that's the cruel reason that I left old Skibbereen.

Oh, well do I remember the bleak December day.
The landlord and the sheriff came to drive us all away.
They set my roof on fire with their cursed English spleen,
And that's another reason that I left old Skibbereen.

Your mother, too, God rest her soul, fell on the snowy ground
She fainted in her anguish, seeing the desolation 'round.
She never rose, but passed away from life to mortal dream,
And found a quiet grave, my boy, in dear old Skibbereen.

And you were only two years old, and feeble was your frame.
I could not leave you with my friends, you bore your father's name—
I wrapped you in my cotamore at the dead of night unseen,
I heaved a sigh and bade good-bye, to dear old Skibbereen.

Oh, father dear, the day may come when in answer to the call,
Each Irishman, with feeling stern, will rally one and all.
I'll be the man to lead the van beneath the flag of green,
When loud and high we'll raise the cry—"Remember Skibbereen."

As the Irish potato crops failed and small farms fell deep in debt, British landholders were quick to evict tenant farmers, hoping to consolidate their fields into larger tracts suitable for grain and livestock production.

this food beyond port towns was not developed. Furthermore, British leaders felt that it would be a grave error to allow the Irish to become dependent on the free distribution of food.

However, the means were found to move the food these farmers had grown for export to the ports of Ireland—usually under armed guard. Food that could have fed the starving millions of Irish was loaded onto ships for British and European markets. British leaders felt there could be no interference in the system of free trade. The journalist Robert Kee tallied the food shipped out of Cork Harbor on November 18, 1848. He noted 147 containers of bacon, 120 casks and 135 barrels of pork, 5 casks of ham, 300 bags of flour, 300 heads of cattle, 239 sheep, and 542 boxes of eggs. While the Irish tried to sustain themselves by eating grass, loads of food left their shores to be sold for British profit.

EVICTION AND STARVATION

With the crop failure, tenants were unable to pay back rents, and many were evicted from their homes. Police or landlords' employees piled the meager belongings of the family in the middle of their yard and nailed shut the door. If the poor tenants tried to re-enter their homes, the walls were pulled down and the thatched roof set on fire. Men and women, too weak from hunger to fight back, meekly gathered up what they could salvage and left their homes. All along the rock walls bordering the fields, families constructed "scalpeens." These lean-to shelters were made up of scavenged thatch roofing that were propped against the wall as a shelter. Other families dug pits called "scalps" in the ground and covered them with a thatch or turf roof to protect themselves from the weather. Parents and children scoured the countryside hoping to find something edible. Berries, grass, and even weeds were eaten in the hope of gleaning nourishment. The weeds and grass, however, were inedible and caused vomiting, which further weakened the starving people and brought them closer to death. Accounts of the dead mention the corpses' green-stained mouths. Without a steady diet, these displaced families were susceptible to illness. Typhus, cholera, and dysentery took hold of the Irish population.

WORKHOUSES

Many evicted families turned to workhouses as their only source of income and food. However, there was not enough space for all the displaced families, and fights broke out as people tried to secure relief jobs in the workhouse. Those who were admitted were separated from their families in barracks, often bedding down where a previous workhouse inmate may have died of fever only moments before. Crowded conditions and deplorable sanitary conditions did nothing to stem the spread of illness. Most men and women were too debilitated by hunger and disease to be of much use on the work crews. Yet, by the unusually cold winter of 1846–47, more than 700,000 people worked for relief assistance. They were put to work breaking rock into gravel with hammers or hauling baskets of gravel to cover roadways. Many fainted or even died on the work site, since relief pay would purchase only one meal a day for their families. Often, children would go without these meals so their parents could eat to have enough strength to work another day. By spring, these road works were canceled.

ASSISTANCE PROGRAMS

British authorities set up soup kitchens in Ireland, which fed an estimated three million people each day. These assistance programs were expensive and were financed by taxation in England. Parliament, hearing grumblings from the public, decided to amend the poor relief law with the Poor Law Extension Act in 1847. This placed the responsibility of financing relief efforts in the hands of the landlords. The costs of food and wages for the workhouse inmates were a burden to the landlords, who tried to pass on the costs by increasing taxation and rent for any remaining tenants on their estates. Even after converting the evicted farms into larger farms for increased productivity, most estates were not profitable for their owners.

EMIGRATION AFTER THE POTATO FAMINE

Although the potato crop in 1847 was healthy, there had been so few salvageable potatoes available for planting after 1846 that only 20 percent of the population could be fed. New poor laws stated that anyone with access to one-quarter acre of land or more was not eligible for relief; so any tenant who had managed to hold onto their land this long was forced to abandon it to get food. One million Irish entered the workhouse, and another million were served by soup kitchens in 1847. But this left millions without relief. The potato crop in 1848 was nearly a complete loss. The harvests in 1849 through 1852 were repeatedly infected, resulting each year in partial failure. With illness, starvation, and death the only imaginable future for the poor in Ireland, emigration was the only option for survival. From 1845 to 1855, the years collectively called the Potato Famine, 1 million Irish men, women, and children died. Another estimated 1.5 million people fled Ireland for the United States and Canada.

CHAPTER

3 SHIPS TO SALVATION

PREPARING TO LEAVE HOME

By 1840, just a few years before the Potato Famine struck, more than one million Irish were living abroad. Hundreds of thousands had settled in Great Britain, Europe, and Canada, and hundreds of thousands of Irish were already living in the United States. Nearly every family still in Ireland had family members or friends who had immigrated to another country. Letters from foreign countries not only told of the opportunities awaiting those who left Ireland, but helped many Irish men and women grow accustomed to the idea of living away from their beloved homeland. For the Irish people, who often had very limited education and life experience outside their small towns and villages, these letters provided a broader world view—a view that didn't seem too frightening. The notion of packing a few belongings and

For the starving Irish, deciding to immigrate to America was often far easier than raising the cost of passage. Many were forced to travel as cheaply as possible, huddling in steerage, or on the unsheltered decks of cargo vessels.

walking out the door for the last time did not seem quite as frightening when they knew that so many of their neighbors had already done so successfully. They also knew there would be familiar faces to meet them on their arrival.

At this same time, international trade between England and the United States was increasing, which made numerous ships available for passage. A typical ship captain brought a ship laden with goods from Canada or the United States to England, but often could not find enough cargo to fill his hold for the return trip across the Atlantic. Transporting passengers in the below-deck steerage area filled this need. The competition for passengers among ships brought ticket prices down during the 1830s and 1840s, which made the decision to immigrate more feasible for many poverty-stricken Irish.

Another factor that led many Irish emigrants to the United States was the excitement surrounding the California Gold Rush of 1849. Accounts of gold nuggets waiting to be picked up off the ground drew so many Irish immigrants westward that by 1870, they grew to be the largest foreign-born group in the state. Even for those who did not pursue the dream of gold, America held the promise of ample job opportunities. The same industrialization of labor that was forcing them out of jobs in Ireland would provide them with employment in their new country. The image of America's riches had been fostered by letters from previous Irish immigrants. When combined with the notion of the United States being the "home of liberty," this provided strong incentive to attempt the Atlantic passage.

GETTING THE FARES FOR PASSAGE

Making the decision to leave was often a simple one since staying in Ireland meant sure starvation. Saving enough money to finance the trip proved to be far more difficult for most Irish families. Trans-Atlantic ships did have some passenger compartments, but at fares between 12 and 15 pounds (approximately \$60 to \$75 at the time), these staterooms were designed to be used by the wealthy traveling between Europe and the United States on holiday trips. These were not the accommodations used by the masses of Famine emigrants. These destitute men and women traveled in steerage, the cargo areas below decks, which were hastily converted for passenger use.

By the 1830s, fares for steerage passage ranged from 3 pounds 10 shillings ($17 to $18) departing from Liverpool, England, to 2 pounds 5 shillings ($11 to $12) leaving from one of Ireland's minor port cities. For families who could not feed or clothe their children, this sum was a small fortune, especially when they tallied the fare for the entire family. Even before the Famine years, it could take years to save the amount needed for fares overseas. With the depressed conditions after the crop failures, cash was nearly impossible to come by.

For many families, salvation arrived by international mail. Letters from previous emigrants, though valued for their news of departed relatives, were doubly important when accompanied by cash. Wages earned in the United States financed approximately one-third to one-half of pre-Famine fares. By 1850, 75 percent of tickets for Atlantic crossings were bought with American earnings or were pre-purchased in the United States.

For a few desperately poor families, planning for emigration was taken out of their hands by their landlords. Faced with enormous tax burdens, the landlords found it cheaper to buy passage aboard for their tenants than to support them either on their properties or in their workhouses. An estimated 50,000 tenants received some sort of "aid" from their landlords, but it was frequently in the form of a combined eviction and emigration. Most landlords could not even free up enough assets to finance emigration, so relatively few Irish were sent abroad this way. Even so, the landlords that did provide passage for the farmers on their land cleared hundreds of people off their property in a relatively short time period.

Entire communities were emptied because of purely economic decisions. For these emigrants, passage was usually provided to Canada rather than the United States. Canada was a colony of England at the time, and government leaders

Coffin Ships to Canada

Some British landlords chose to pay for their tenants' passage abroad rather than support them on their Irish estates or in the workhouse. This was often a cheaper solution and the only way for the landlords to avoid financial ruin. The ships they chartered were usually destined for Canada, a less expensive destination than cities in the United States. The landlords often selected older and, therefore, cheaper, ships to make the passage. Many of these ships earned the name "coffin ships" for the number of emigrants who died in the crossing and for the cramped size of the steerage berths.

Major Dennis Mahon, a landlord in County Roscommon, realized in 1847 that he was not far from financial ruin. His accountants noted that it cost much less to send one pauper to the United States or Canada than to keep him in the workhouse. By their accounts, two-thirds of the tenants would have to be evicted to make the estate profitable again.

Mahon sent 500 men, women, and children to Québec, Canada, that summer and evicted an additional 500 tenants at a later date on the chartered ships *Virginius* and *Naomi*. The *Virginius* arrived in August at the quarantine station located on Grosse Isle, 30 miles east of Québec City. It was staffed by superintendent Dr. George Douglas and three nurses. Of the 476 passengers who set sail from Liverpool, 158 had died during the voyage, and 106 were ill on arrival. Douglas reported that no more than six or eight of the passengers were really healthy. The *Naomi* arrived soon afterward. Of its original 331 passengers, 78 died at sea and 104 were sick with typhus. Dr. Douglas' report stated, "The filth and dirt in this vessel's hold create such an effluvium [offensive smell] as to make it difficult to breathe." As news of these numerous deaths reached family and friends remaining in Ireland, understandable resentment built up against Major Mahon. Six months after the departure of the *Virginius* and *Naomi* from Ireland, Major Mahon was assassinated.

The station at Grosse Isle welcomed some of the worst casualties of Irish emigration in 1847, when an estimated one out of six passengers died. It is estimated that as many as 15,000 men, women, and children died after being admitted, or waiting to be admitted, to the hospital at Grosse Isle. Today, a 50-foot Celtic cross, with inscriptions in English, French, and Gaelic, stands as a monument dedicated to the thousands who died at Grosse Isle.

actually encouraged settlement of this largely uninhabited region. Most of the Irish passengers, however, planned to cross to the United States as soon as possible to reunite with friends and relatives already living there.

On the morning of departure, relatives and friends from the local community would gather to say their farewells to the emigrant family, often weeping bitterly. Most of them would never see each other again. This feeling of permanent separation was reflected in the Gaelic terms they used. Emigration was called *deoraí*, which strictly translated means "exile." The emigrants themselves, called the *dibeartach*, were "banished people." Handshakes and embraces, often accompanied by whatever coins that could be spared, were pressed on the emigrants as they said good-bye.

GETTING TO PORT

Often, the journey to America began on foot—or at best in a small cart—toward the nearest port city and the Atlantic crossing. What few belongings the family owned and deemed worth saving, such as some bedding or cooking items, were tied in parcels and carried. Most often the emigrants took only what clothes they were wearing and what food they could scrape together—usually just a bag of potatoes.

Because of the difference in fares, most emigrants hoped to depart for America from an Irish port. However, Ireland did not draw much import/export traffic other than with England. There was simply not enough ship traffic to handle the numbers of desperate emigrants wanting passage. Departures from Irish ports averaged between 20,000 and 30,000 people annually up until 1855. Each year, roughly 7,000 emigrants left from both the main port cities of Cork and Limerick, with 3,500 leaving from each minor port, such as Sligo, Derry, Belfast, New Ross, and Waterford. Other Irish ports included Dublin, Donegal, and Wexford.

WAITING FOR A SHIP

Few of these ships sailed directly to the United States from Ireland. Indeed, the desire of the passenger to make a quick start for America was not a guiding factor. The trade route of each particular ship determined the path the emigrant would take. Ships calling at Limerick, Ireland, had brought timber from Québec City or St. Johns in Canada. Derry was frequented by ships from Philadelphia bringing flour or maize. Most ships called at Liverpool before they returned to Canada. Many more ships headed to Liverpool without stopping at an Irish port. These ships were on routes that had begun in New York City, where manufactured goods or coal were loaded for transport to southern cities. These cargoes were unloaded in New Orleans, Mobile, Savannah, or Charleston and replaced with cotton from plantations throughout the South. The cotton was brought to Liverpool, where Irish emigrants fought one another for jobs unloading these 500-pound bales and fought again for space as human cargo.

WAITING AGAIN IN LIVERPOOL

In Liverpool, the emigrants were joined by thousands of passengers who could not find a place on a ship bound from Ireland and had crossed the Irish Sea to embark for America. This additional leg in their journey delayed their departure, sometimes for weeks, and added to their cost of travel. The smaller boats crossing between Dublin and Liverpool charged passengers about five shillings for a space on deck. The emigrant was forced to stand and be exposed to the weather, crowded against his fellow passengers for the 24- to 36-hour trip. The protected space below deck was set aside for the valuable food exports these same Irish families had nearly died to produce. The cost of the crossing to Liverpool, the price of lodging while waiting for a ship, and additional passage money for the increased fare from England raised these emigrants' expenses to five to seven pounds.

The wait for a ship bound for America could be lengthy, and many boarding-houses sprung up around Liverpool, England's Waterloo docks. This drawing depicts a desperate crowd of men, women, and children boarding a ship at Waterloo docks.

The difficulties of the journey began before the emigrant was able to leave Liverpool. Passengers were not allowed to board the ships until the last minute and therefore had to wait for their ships' departure along the docks. Innumerable boarding houses formed a slum area among the warehouses and charged high prices for food and lodging. People crowded into the available lodgings, not only making themselves susceptible to theft among the throngs of people, but also adding to the filthy conditions within. This, in turn, led to the spread of disease, dangerous to the emigrants who were already in weakened states because of malnutrition.

DISEASE AND DEATH

Although emigrants were supposed to undergo a health inspection before being allowed on board a ship, many did not because of the lack of available medical inspectors. The inspections that were carried out were brief, and only the most obviously ill emigrants were prevented from boarding. Emigrants denied passage on the first ship due to illness desperately sought to find available spaces on the next departing ship and were often victims of swindlers who sold false tickets on nonexistent vessels.

SHIP IMPROVEMENTS

The transport of passengers was seen by ship's captains as a necessary evil. Although the passage fares provided a profit, since the ship had to make the return journey with or without cargo, it added a burden for the crew. The 1842 United Kingdom Passenger Act required cargo areas to have some accommodations to make them suitable for human transport. Ships had to be retrofitted (modification or installation of new parts) with bunks for the emigrants, and additional regulations and restrictions had to be followed. Some of these included providing water and food for the emigrants or providing cooking facilities for the preparation of the food they brought with them.

DANGEROUS CROSSINGS

The press of desperate Irish families during the late 1840s changed the traditional season for emigration against the better judgment of many ships' crews. Throughout history, the typical season for the trans-Atlantic crossing from Ireland was from March to June, when stormy winter conditions had calmed. This remained the case through 1846, for the blight did not strike until the summer months. The suffering that ensued convinced many not to wait until spring to leave home, and 1846–1847 saw the first winter crossing from Ireland. Thereafter, year-round emigration became the norm for the duration of the Famine.

The decision to leave in winter was not made lightly, for even in good weather the small wooden ships were susceptible to fires and sinking. The poor weather added to the duration of the trip as well. The journey, which took a month under good conditions, could take as much as two or three months because of storms or unfavorable winds. Between 1847 and 1853, 59 ships bearing emigrants to Canada or the United States were lost at sea.

CONDITIONS ON BOARD

Even with these drawbacks in mind, the emigrants eagerly awaited the day of departure. Boarding amid the confusion of the crew preparing to set sail, emigrant families were met with barely habitable conditions for their journey. Most of the ships were small, with steerage space dimensions typically measuring 75 by 25 feet. The overhead deck was often so low that only a child could stand upright. A few oil lamps were the only lighting provided below decks, and these were extinguished when ocean conditions got rough for fear that a lamp would fall over and start a fire. Some cargo was stored within this hold, and the remainder of the space was filled with glorified shelving that would serve as bunks for the emigrant travelers. The berths were often shared by four or more passengers—frequently complete strangers to one another—who had to sleep in shifts.

No division of the area was made for separate men's and women's quarters. The steerage area was unbelievably crowded, and many people spent most of their time during the passage lying in these bunks. In addition, the ship's crew made no

Rather than have their cargo ships return empty to America, shipping companies agreed to transport passengers as a way of generating revenue. With passengers crowded into cargo holds outfitted with makeshift wooden bunks, the transatlantic voyage was difficult for many Irish immigrants. This drawing shows women and children in one such makeshift set of bunks.

provisions for sanitary or private toilets. This became more than an inconvenience as the journey progressed and added to the spread of illness on board. The following description of steerage conditions in emigrant ships during the Potato Famine appeared in the London *Times* newspaper:

> The emigrant is shown a berth, a shelf of coarse pinewood, situated in a noisome dungeon, airless and lightless, in which several hundred persons of both sexes and all ages are stowed away on shelves two feet one inch above the other, three feet wide and six feet long, still reeking from the ineradicable stench left by the emigrants of the last voyage.

The small ships were affected more strongly by waves on the ocean, and most of the emigrants were violently seasick at the outset of the trip. This resulted in the floor of the hold (the ship's interior below deck) soon being covered in vomit. The only ventilation came from the one or two hatchways from the deck, which were left open only during good weather. Steerage conditions became increasingly dirty and foul as the trip progressed, and lice were commonplace. Seasickness left the passengers weakened and wasted much of their food supply. Malnutrition and disease had been constant companions to the emigrants even before they left their homes in Ireland and throughout their stopover in Liverpool. These horrors would not desert them during the trip.

Although United States Passengers' Acts held the ship responsible for providing water and some food for the passengers, these were often present in name only. Six pints of water per day was to be given to each passenger to drink, wash, and cook. If the trip was delayed by bad weather, this ration was often cut short. The ship was required to give each person only one pound of food each day: usually bread, biscuits, flour, rice, oatmeal, or potatoes. In many cases, water became unsanitary and disease ridden. Food supplies were often rancid, and one or two small cooking fires were expected to be shared by hundreds of passengers. People usually ate raw what little food they had, however, given that the open flames were permitted in calm weather only.

Passengers were allowed on deck during fine weather only—and then in small groups—so there was very little relief from the crowded, stinking steerage compartment. Weakened by their near-starvation, there was little gaiety. Illnesses such as typhus, cholera, and dysentery, brought aboard from Ireland or the slums of Liverpool's waterfront swept the ships. There was never sufficient medicine to adequately treat the sick, and no way for others to avoid contamination. During storms, the steerage compartment was sealed until the weather passed, and any passengers who died waited among the living for the hold to be opened by the crew.

Because of these factors, the mortality rate was very high for Famine emigrants. Mortality rates vary according to the annual numbers of passengers, but overall, the death rate averaged 5 to 12 percent for the Irish who boarded what they thought were ships for their salvation. The worst year was 1847, when rampant disease claimed nearly 20 percent of all U.S. bound Irish emigrants—at least 40,000 people.

Sadly, as the Great Famine lasted from 1845 to 1855, technology and invention did not advance rapidly enough in the nineteenth century to aid the Famine emigrants. After the Famine, by the late 1850s, ships were being designed and built specifically for the emigrant trade, and steam engines had replaced the sailing ships for power. These ships were far more comfortable, with adequate space and sanitary facilities for those on board, greatly reducing the incidence and spread of illness. Passenger ticket prices dropped to an average of four to six pounds, comparable to the earlier steerage prices. Steam power greatly increased the speed of the ship, reducing the duration of the trip to 10 to 14 days on average, making malnutrition en route a thing of the past.

SHARED DETERMINATION TO BETTER THEMSELVES

Even facing the deplorable conditions of their travel space, weakened by disease and lack of food, and facing an unknown future in a strange country, the Irish emigrants shared a number of characteristics. The primary one was poverty. These families had lived their entire lives in ragged clothing, living under primitive conditions and subsisting on a meager diet. Most had always been rural dwellers and had no experience living in the towns or cities of Ireland. Though destitute, the emigrants often viewed arrival in the United States as a new opportunity for a better life than what they had left behind. The second characteristic they had in common was their hatred of the British, whom they held responsible for much of the hardship they had faced in Ireland. Most of the emigrants shared their Catholic faith, which gave many of them the strength, hope, and drive to succeed in America.

LANDING

More than 1.5 million Irish men, women, and their children came to North America during the Potato Famine. Most of them caught their first sight of America off the East Coast as they approached the ports of New York, Boston, Philadelphia, or Baltimore. In fact, by 1845, three-fourths of immigrants to America entered through New York City. Other ships veered toward Canada, where St. John's, Newfoundland, was their first glimpse of land after weeks or months at sea. Still others headed for the ports of the South, such as New Orleans or Savannah. Many of these families who landed at Canadian and southern locations did not plan to stay there. They had merely gotten to America by whatever means possible and planned to migrate to New England and the mid-Atlantic states to join their families.

There was no immigrant processing station available at these various ports to meet the Famine emigrants. Most truly

Upon their arrival in New York City, Irish and other immigrants had to endure a lengthy registration process that included a medical examination and customs check. Here, we see the Great Hall at Ellis Island, through which millions of immigrants passed before the facility's closing in 1954.

had to fend for themselves upon arrival. As ships bound for New York City approached the harbor, they first stopped at Staten Island for medical examinations. Sick passengers were unloaded and placed under quarantine, separating family members from one another. Those declared healthy remained on board ship and proceeded on to the port. The quarantine station at Staten Island became so filthy and run down that local residents living nearby complained frequently about the conditions. When no improvements were made, the frustrated neighbors rioted and burned it down in 1858, fearing a yellow fever epidemic.

LATER LANDING STATIONS

The state immigration center at Castle Garden would not open until 1855, just as the final waves of Famine Irish were entering the United States. About 70 percent of all immigrants to the United States landed here, including more than two million Irish men and women. There, the immigrants received medical examinations, went through customs, and were registered as having entered the country. Immigrants also found job information, learned where to find lodging, exchanged their money for American currency, and could even have letters written and sent to their families.

New York's federal immigration center at Ellis Island would not be completed until 1892. The first official immigrant through Ellis Island was 15-year-old Annie Moore, who arrived with her younger brother from County Cork, Ireland. An additional million Irish immigrants followed Annie's path, entering the United States through Ellis Island until it closed in 1954.

CHAPTER

4

FOOTSTEPS ON A NEW SHORE

The moment he landed, his luggage was pounced upon by two runners, one seizing the box of tools, the other confiscating the clothes. The future American citizen assured his obliging friends that he was quite capable of carrying his own luggage. But no, they should relieve him . . . of that trouble. Each [represented] a different boarding house, and each insisted that the young Irishman . . . should go with him. . . . Not being able to oblige both gentlemen, he could oblige only one; and as the tools were more valuable than the clothes, he followed in the path of the gentleman who had secured that portion of the "plunder."

New York City reporter describing a typical immigrant arrival in the 1840s

NEW ARRIVALS JOIN EARLIER IMMIGRANTS

Most of the Famine immigrants had no official welcome to the United States. If the family had been lucky enough to notify relatives of the name of their ship before leaving Ireland or Liverpool, they may have been met by friendly faces who had a spare room to share until they could find work and a permanent place to live. Even so, immigrants were met by the clamor and bustle of the largest collection of people they had ever seen in their lives. New York City had more than 500,000 inhabitants

Unless they had the time and resources to notify family members in America, Irish immigrants arriving in New York City received no official welcome. Instead they found themselves seeking employment in a crowded and unfamiliar city, filled with pickpockets and con artists. This painting from the 1800s shows Irish immigrants arriving at New York Harbor.

in 1850, far more than in any Irish city. This was a bewildering, frightening, and disheartening experience for most immigrants. Weak, hungry, and homesick, they gathered their few belongings together and disembarked from the ship. At that point, they huddled dockside, confused as to what to do next.

Pickpockets and con artists found the recent arrivals easy targets. "Runners" were notorious for stealing the immigrant's luggage and leading them to a boarding house, where exorbitant rates were charged for rooms. Many of the Irish were victims of thieves who claimed to be employment agents holding jobs (nonexistent, of course) for them in exchange for a modest fee. There were also the ticket agents who sold overpriced or false tickets to the immigrants. The New York state legislature did set up a commission to deal with some of these problems in 1847. A new hospital housed those who were ill or malnourished after the trip, and city regulations were passed to try to keep the new arrivals from being exploited. Some Irish families simply had nothing to steal and had to find shelter at almshouses for the poor. However, most Famine immigrants did have relatives or neighbors from Ireland who had arrived in America before them. Reuniting with familiar faces eased the transition of the new arrivals to their home.

AMERICAN-IRISH POPULATION GROWTH

By the 1840s, the United States already held a considerable Irish immigrant population. In fact, just before the huge influx of Famine immigrants, there were already an estimated 415,000 Irish living in the United States. The indentured servants who arrived during the colonial era were joined by Northern Irish settlers who helped carve out the American frontier after the American Revolution. By the turn of the century, Irish immigrants could be found throughout the United States. The construction of the canal system, which reached its high point in the 1820s and 1830s, employed tens of thousands of Irish workers, many directly recruited in Ireland. This pre-industrial

My America

In the excerpted letter below, Irish immigrant Margaret MCarthy relates her experiences as an Irish immigrant in the nineteenth century to her family back in County Cork, Ireland. This letter has been reprinted with respect to its original spelling and punctuation.

New York September 22nd, 1850

My Dr. Father and Mother Brothers and Sisters,

I write these few lines to you hopeing That these few lines may find you all in as good State of health as I am at present. . . . My Dr. Father I must only say that this is a good place and A good Country for if one place does not Suit A man he can go to Another and can very easy please himself But there is one thing thats Ruining this place Especially the Frontirs towns and Cities where the flow of Emmigration is most the Emmigrants has not money enough to Take them to the Interior of the Country which oblidges them to Remain here in New York and the like places for which Reason Causes the less demand for Labour and also the great Reduction in wages for this Reason I would advise no one to Come to America that would not have Some Money after landing here that (would) Enable them to go west in case they would get no work to do here but any man or woman without a family are fools that would not venture and Come to this plentyful Country where no man or woman ever Hungerd or ever will and where you will not be Seen Naked, but I can asure you there are Dangers upon Dangers Attending Comeing here but my Friends nothing Venture nothing have Fortune will favour the brave have Courage. . . and Come you all Together Couragiously and bid adieu to that lovely place the land of our Birth. that place where the young and old joined Together in one Common Union, both night and day Engaged in Innocent Amusement, But alas. I am now Told its the Gulf of Misersry oppression Degradetion and Ruin of evry Discription which I am Sorry to hear of so Doleful a History to Be told of our Dr. Country. . . .

When you are Comeing do not be frightened Take Courage and be Determined in your Undertaking as the first two or three days will be the worst to you and mind whatever happens on board Keep your own temper and do not speak angry to any or hasty the Mildest Man has the best chance on board. . . .

Your Ever Dear and Loveing Child.
Margaret MCarthy

Many Irish immigrants found work as laborers, helping to build America's network of canals that connected the industrial cities of the East with the Great Lakes of the Midwest. Though canal building meant backbreaking labor for little pay, the Irish proved themselves up to the task.

transportation system opened up 4,000 miles of quick, cheap routes to move goods and travelers and led to the further dispersion of Irish immigrants across America.

The canals joined the northeastern states of New York and Pennsylvania to the southwestern Great Lakes region and the Mississippi River system through Ohio and into Illinois. As the canals progressed west, workers formed Irish shantytowns that later grew into small towns across the region. Other men opted for a more settled lifestyle when the canals were completed and chose to bring their families to reside in midwestern cities.

CITY VERSUS RURAL LIVING

Most of the Irish in the United States resided in cities. Unlike many other immigrant groups in the late nineteenth century, the Catholic Irish did not come to America intending to buy their own farmland. Lack of money was the main reason for this; few Irish immigrants could afford to travel to interior states and purchase acreage, tools, and equipment. Even land priced cheaply to attract settlement was beyond the means of the Famine Irish. Also, farming did not attract the interest of many Irish immigrants. Even those who had worked on farms in Ireland had only been laborers. They did not have a background in the business side of farming.

Also, farming held bad associations for most of the immigrants. They had nearly died trying to farm in Ireland, and there was no guarantee that things would be any different here in America. The farming communities in America were also different from what they had been used to in Ireland. Instead of having many families grouped together to farm small plots of land, a single family here worked on a vast property, often without any neighbors in sight. This isolation did not appeal to the Irish immigrants. Fewer than 10 percent of Famine immigrants settled in rural areas.

ASSISTANCE SOCIETIES

As more of their countrymen arrived throughout the 1800s, established Irish immigrants formed Hibernian societies and assistance agencies to help the new arrivals find work and housing and connect to the existing Irish community in many cities. These organizations date back to 1737, when the Charitable Irish Society of Boston began to give aid to their fellow Irish "who may be reduced by Sickness, Shipwrack [*sic*], Old age and other Infirmities and unforseen [*sic*] Accidents. . . ." In Philadelphia, the Hibernian Society for the Relief of Emigrants from Ireland began in 1790, and a similar group formed in Savannah in 1812.

The huge population of Irish immigrants in New York City could turn to many agencies, such as the Emigrant Assistance Society, formed in 1825. Perhaps most notable was the Irish Emigrant Society, founded in 1841. This organization developed the Emigrant Savings Bank in 1850. Irish families could open savings accounts to be used for the purchase of future passage tickets for members of their families who remained in Ireland. Thousands of Irish immigrants held accounts in the bank, which remained open until 1880.

WHERE THEY SETTLED

Most Irish men and women who arrived during the Famine years had no extra money when they landed in America. Often sick and weak from their journey, they had to take whatever employment was available close at hand and settled for the cheapest housing they could find. These were the determining factors in Irish settlement patterns in the United States. This resulted in most of the Famine population staying in the eastern seaboard cities where they had landed. The arrival of the Irish immigrants coincided with the industrialization of labor in the United States, and the expanding textile mills, factories, and mining operations quickly incorporated the unskilled Irish laborers into their workforce. Much of this industry was centered in the North, near port cities where manufactured goods could easily be exported.

To meet the labor demands, most of the Irish immigrants settled along New England's coast from Maine to Long Island, New York. Irish-born immigrants made up 25 percent of the populations of New York City and Boston in 1860 and 16 percent of the population of Philadelphia. The Famine immigrants settled most heavily in New York City, and by 1860 roughly 13 percent of all Irish-born men and women in the entire country lived there.

The Midwest continued to draw a significant number of Irish immigrants, many rejoining relatives who had previously settled there. Canal and railroad work camps had grown into small towns and cities, many still retaining an Irish heritage. By 1850, St. Louis, Cincinnati, and Detroit all held between

12 and 15 percent of Irish-born residents. Chicago held even more; by 1870, its 40,000 Irish residents made it the city with the fourth-largest Irish population in the country. Irish community leaders in the East tried to establish colonies of Irish immigrants in the Midwest during the 1850s and 1860s, and several successful settlements were founded in Minnesota and Nebraska.

At times, the only jobs that were available took the Irish laborer away from the rest of his family in the eastern cities. Many men enlisted in the army during the Mexican-American War from 1846 to 1848, where they could receive three meals a day plus a wage they could send home to their family. The war's outcome gained additional territory for the United States, which lured some of the Irish immigrants westward. The California Gold Rush, stemming from the discovery at Sutter's Mill in 1848, enticed others. The development of the transcontinental railroad during the 1850s and 1860s brought Irish workers out of the crowded eastern cities to build rail lines across the entire country. San Francisco was the most concentrated settlement in the West, with nearly 26,000 Irish residents by 1870.

Only about 10 percent of Famine immigrants settled in southern states, where the heavily agricultural society depended on slave labor instead. Many had arrived in the port cities of New Orleans, Charleston, and Baltimore, and these areas held the greatest number of Irish in the south in the 1860s. Richmond, Savannah, and Memphis also became home to immigrants in the South. Some of the immigrants then traveled by boat up the Mississippi River to reach midwestern cities. Many of the Irish who had landed in these southern cities immediately left to travel to the Middle Atlantic and New England states to reunite with relatives. They were frequently told by corrupt ticket agents in England and Ireland that these locations were a mere two- or three-day walk from the cities of the South.

As immigrants flowed rapidly into New York City, tenement neighborhoods sprang up. Far different from the small thatched cottages to which the Irish were accustomed, these noisy and crowded apartment buildings challenged the resilience of even the heartiest Irish immigrants.

IRISH COMMUNITIES FORM

For the Irish immigrant family, settling in America was an enormous transition. Most felt cut off and set adrift from the close ties of community and family they had left behind. They were homesick and felt that they had been forced to leave. This shared emotional exile was largely responsible for the Irish immigrants banding together so closely after they had reached America. By living together in Irish communities they tried to recreate some of their own Irish customs and culture. However, even living with fellow Irish immigrants, the noisy, crowded tenements (apartment houses meeting minimum standards) were far different from their thatched cottages in the Irish countryside. Rather than spending their lives surrounded by a small group of close family and friends, they found themselves in huge cities among hundreds of thousands of strangers.

The lifestyle of the average Irish immigrant changed instantly from that of a rural agricultural laborer, who toiled according to the natural dictates of the weather and harvests, to an urban factory worker, controlled by schedules, production quotas, and the time clock. Though work hours were usually very long and wages were low, most immigrants felt it was preferable to starving to death in Ireland.

CHAPTER

5 NO IRISH NEED APPLY

It is time to speak of ourselves. I have been much disheartened since my arrival here by the unfortunate condition of my countrymen. I came with high hopes and sanguine expectations, and I have realized my disappointment. . . . Religious bigotry and party feuds have crossed the Atlantic with our people. Our nature has not changed with the clime. . . . What I state of the Irish in America is fact, and it is foolish or criminal to conceal it. Their position is not what it is represented to be at home—far different; it is one of shame and poverty. They are shunned and despised. The name of Irish politics is anathema, and Ireland is as much a subject of contempt as pity. "My master is a great tyrant," said a negro lately, "he treats me as badly as if I was a common Irishman."

Joseph Brennan, in a letter in 1850

Although America promised great opportunity to Irish immigrants, anti-Irish prejudice was in no short supply. As this cartoon's unflattering portrait of "Paddy" the Irish hod carrier (bricklayer's assistant) suggests, the Irish were often ridiculed as uneducated, unskilled, and ape-like.

As the Famine immigrants became accustomed to their new society, they quickly realized that America was not the land of opportunity for all, as they had been led to believe. In fact, the Irish were subject to discrimination based on stereotypes that had been formed in the minds of East Coast residents decades before their arrival. The attitudes toward the Irish had been influenced a great deal by earlier Irish settlers. More than

150,000 Irish lived in the United States by 1820, and most shared their Protestant faith with Americans. They also shared their strong work ethic, desire to succeed, and tendency toward temperance. These earlier, wealthier immigrants did not identify with their poorer countrymen fleeing the Famine. By the 1840s, the Ulster natives widely used the term Scots-Irish to distinguish themselves from the southern Catholics settling in America.

After 1820, the numbers of Catholic Irish immigrants rose, prompting fear and mistrust as they constructed separate churches and schools. Prejudice toward Catholics sometimes found violent outlets, as in the 1834 burning of a Catholic convent and school in Charlestown, Massachusetts. A protest in 1844 by Protestants in the Kensington neighborhood of Philadelphia who opposed the use of a Catholic version of the Bible led to riots that lasted two months and resulted in the deaths of 13 people and the destruction of two Catholic churches. Conveniently forgetting that their own ancestors came to America from foreign nations, "nativist" (a person who believes that there should be no immigrants in a country) politicians warned that the Irish would weaken the ethnic unity of the nation. Their Catholic religion was seen as a threat, as it was feared that the immigrants would pay more attention to a foreign pope rather than attach their loyalty to their adoptive nation.

DISCRIMINATION AGAINST THE IRISH IMMIGRANTS

Catholicism was only one characteristic that brought scorn upon the Irish. Most were used to rural living, and their rough, outdated clothing caused them to stand out plainly on city streets. Their tendency to turn to alcohol and violence to ease their frustrations earned them a reputation as savage drunks. As industrialization revolutionized labor, the social structure of its citizens changed as the privileged elite formed class distinctions based on wealth. With little education and no professional experience, Irish men and women were limited to jobs as unskilled laborers, setting them apart from the wealthy upper class and skilled professionals of the middle class. In the North, this put them in direct competition with free blacks for positions that demanded long hours and low pay. Most of their employers saw the Irish as unsuitable for anything but menial jobs and would not consider them for many positions. Job advertisements in newspapers and placards in shop windows sometimes warned, "No Irish Need Apply." One example was found in the *Daily Sun* newspaper on May 11, 1853: "Woman wanted—to do general housework . . . English, Scotch, Welsh, German, or any country or color except Irish."

Although their own discrimination limited the types of jobs and the salaries Irish immigrants could earn, the American Protestants still found fault with the Irish for not "getting ahead" economically or socially. Since many Irish families were sending any spare wages home to relatives in Ireland to pay debts and purchase passage fees, they continued to live in the worst slums in the northern cities, which promoted the stereotype that they were a lazy and uncivilized race.

COMPETITION WITH BLACKS FOR WORK

In the South, Irish immigrants found themselves placed in an odd position within the rigid socioeconomic hierarchy. Although they were white, their foreign origin placed them socially below the poorest white planter. In New Orleans, the Irish lived in the swampy lowlands along a ditch called the Irish Channel and worked there digging drainage canals. Plantation owners chose to hire the Irish workers at a wage rather than risk their slaves as workers because of the high risk of injury or contracting malaria in the humid, mosquito-ridden area. One Southern writer remarked, "the niggers are worth too much to be risked here; if the Paddies are knocked overboard or get their backs broke, nobody loses anything."

The competition extended to the waterfront area, where gangs of Irish men fought black laborers for jobs loading and unloading ship cargo. The struggle for employment led to animosity and racial rivalry; indeed, most Irish did not favor the emancipation of slaves during the Civil War. They feared abolition would flood the market with a huge supply of unskilled laborers, a population of nearly 4 million men, women, and children with whom they would have to compete for their livelihood and survival.

IRISHTOWNS

American discrimination against the Irish, when combined with their poverty on arrival, resulted in their banding together to support one another in close-knit Irish communities. The 1850 census for the Irish Five Points neighborhood of New York City records that 75 percent of the immigrants came in family groups or met relatives on arrival. About 86 percent lived with at least one relative by blood or marriage, and 93 percent lived in nuclear family households. Of the unmarried men and women who did not live with relatives, only 5 percent roomed in boarding houses, most preferring to board with a family instead.

Often, families from common towns or counties in Ireland grouped together again in American cities, drawing strength and support from familiar faces and voices in the streets around them. Upper Mulberry Street in New York housed immigrants from Sligo, whereas the lower blocks were taken up by natives of Cork. Kerry emigrants lived on Baxter Street. Although the American community would not dream of renting to the Irish in other parts of town, they criticized the immigrants for being "clannish" and "standoffish." Their "Irishtowns" were centered wherever cheap housing could be found. This ended up being the subdivided rooms in ramshackle tenement buildings and cellar apartments in the poorest sections of town. Single rooms in boarding houses held up to a dozen or more people, and tenements

Irish-American communities sprang up wherever cheap housing could be found. New York City's Mulberry Street neighborhood housed families who had emigrated from the Irish counties of Sligo and Cork, while Baxter Street was home to those from Kerry.

often housed hundreds in a single building. At times, even old factories or warehouses were subdivided into apartments to take advantage of the demand for housing.

Boston's north end near Boston Harbor became the residential zone for Irish immigrants. It quickly became the most densely populated area of the entire city. In New York

City, the Irish settled in lower Manhattan in an area known as Five Points. The hub of this crazy intersection of five streets held a small park optimistically and ironically called Paradise Square. Even before the influx of Famine immigrants, Five Points was known as the worst slum in the United States. It remained a center of settlement for the Irish, however, because rents could be found for as little as $2 a month for a tiny room in a dark, dank cellar apartment.

LIVING CONDITIONS

Tenement amenities (conveniences) were usually limited to a stove for heating and cooking, an unfamiliar appliance for the immigrants who had previously cooked only over an open fire. Apartments had no running water or electricity as yet, and there were frequently no windows in the apartments, making them dark and airless. Single outhouses on the ground floor outside the buildings were used by hundreds of tenants. Garbage was dumped directly into the street, where rats, dogs, and even pigs roamed freely, feeding on the refuse. The filthy, unsafe conditions of the housing was described by Charles Dickens upon his visit to Five Points in 1842:

> What place is this, to which the squalid street conducts us? A kind of square of leprous houses, some of which are attainable only by crazy wooden stairs. . . . Here, too, are lanes and alleys, paved with mud knee-deep: underground chambers, where they dance and game; the walls bedecked rough designs of ships, and forts, and flags, and American Eagles out of number: ruined houses, open to the street, whence, through wide gaps in the walls, other ruins loom upon the eye, as though the world of vice and misery had nothing else to show: hideous tenements which take their name from robbery and murder; all [that] is loathsome, drooping, and decayed is here.

The crowded, unsanitary conditions of these Irish ghettos led to outbreaks of disease. Typhoid fever swept through the

Irish community in 1837, followed by typhus in 1842 and cholera in 1849, affecting thousands of families. Tuberculosis, pneumonia, and dysentery often swept through the Irish community, leading to an average life expectancy of 40 years for the immigrants. Between 1849 and 1859, 85 percent of the foreign patients admitted to Manhattan's Bellevue Hospital were Irish.

By the 1850s, the New York Irish community had moved north to be closer to the dock area, slaughterhouses, and breweries where they worked. Conditions there were no better than at Five Points, and desperate Irish often turned to alcohol and criminal activity in their frustration. More than half the arrests in New York in the 1850s were of Irish men, who were convicted at six times the rate of other Americans. They were usually collared for drunkenness and fighting, thus further promoting the negative stereotypes of the Irish. This era led to the use of the condescending term for police vans as "Paddy wagons," based on the American nickname for Patrick, which was used as a catch-all name for Irish men. This New York waterfront region became known for its violence.

The comments of a team of policemen resulted in the descriptive name for the neighborhood. The younger officer compared the slum to hell, but his older partner responded, "Hell's a mild climate. This is Hell's Kitchen." Even with such deplorable conditions, these slums were preferable to the immigrants' rough cottages in Ireland or the scalpeens where evicted families had lived, hoping to avoid starvation.

OPPORTUNITIES TO EARN A LIVING

After they had found a place for their family to live, Irish men bore the main responsibility of earning a living to support the family. The influx of immigrants provided a huge labor pool of unskilled workers for employers, but also resulted in lower wages for all. In the 1830s, these laborers earned from $1 to

In the late nineteenth century, the New York City neighborhood of Five Points held the dubious distinction of being America's worst slum. Basement lodging houses like the one depicted in this drawing had no running water or electricity.

$1.25 each day. The additional numbers of employees, willing to work for any wage to feed their families, brought the average daily wage down to $0.75 by 1850. This was the wage for men, with women averaging even less, and children earning half an adult's wage for the same number of hours worked. Even with these poor wages, Irish men, women, and children all entered the workforce. This added to the growing animosity of the

American unskilled laborer, who blamed the immigrant for his loss of pay. Working and living conditions were abysmal in many fields, yet there were no labor unions to help ease the suffering of the Irish.

Most men took jobs as day laborers within the city, constantly moving from one short-term construction project to the next. Irish strength and stamina built the foundations of transportation systems in cities across the country, including roads and bridges, and in later years constructed subways, elevated rail lines, buildings, and skyscrapers. Irish crews were predominant in the construction of the pedestal and foundation for the Statue of Liberty, an ironic beginning for the symbol of American freedom and opportunity for later groups of immigrants.

Irish men also found work in the city's stables, slaughterhouses, breweries, and saloons. They also provided muscle at the waterfront as stevedores, who loaded and unloaded ship cargoes, and as draymen, who delivered goods in horse-drawn wagons. Still others worked as tailors and cobblers (shoemakers), or made textiles. Those who could not find work in the cities where their families were settled had to migrate to other parts of the country to earn a living, as they had done in Ireland during the harvest.

CONSTRUCTION OF THE RAILROADS

At mid-century, advances in technology provided the means for new types of employment, and provided a way to escape the slums and discrimination of the eastern cities. The development of the steam engine brought the railroad to the forefront of America's transportation system and mechanized textile mills and factories across New England. With steam power, the locomotive became the favored means of transportation. Canals were forgotten, and thousands of miles of rail lines appeared in all parts of the country. The tens of thousands of Irish men who had previously excavated and leveled canal waterways switched to railroad building. This often kept them away from their families back in eastern cities for months every year. Like canal work, the jobs were dangerous, hours were long, and most work was done with hand tools. Breaking rock with hand picks, shoveling and leveling rail beds, and hand-placing sticks of dynamite for excavation led to numerous accidents and deaths. It was even said that "an Irishman lay buried underneath every railroad tie," a testament to the thousands of Irish workers who connected the Atlantic and Pacific coasts in the 1850s.

These Irish workers were often treated poorly by their bosses. In 1853, a group of Irish workers on the Erie Railroad went on strike in the hope of settling on a 10-hour day and earning a daily wage of $1.25. The strike was not successful. Projects were abandoned when money ran out, stranding the workers at the end of the line. Pay was sometimes delayed for months, or men were paid with IOUs or whiskey. This was not sufficient for men whose families, left behind in New York or Boston, were waiting for their wages. It was even worse for men whose families traveled with them, living in shanties beside the tracks, with no other source of income available. Violence broke out frequently, and many workers turned to alcohol in their frustration. Unfortunately, as the rail lines stretched across the United States, the behaviors of the Irish workers were seen and perceived by the public as typically Irish, further promoting the discrimination felt by the Irish nationwide.

COAL MINING

Railroad jobs also allowed many immigrants, and sometimes their families as well, to relocate to other parts of the country where they found other employment. Mining became another typically Irish job. Like railroad work, mining was performed for long hours and low pay. Irish men excavated ore across the country from the coal mines in Pennsylvania to copper mines in Montana, silver mines in Nevada, and gold in the Black Hills,

How Others Saw Them

Queen Victoria, after a visit to Ireland during the Famine, observed in her journal that the Irish were a ". . . more ragged and wretched people than I ever saw anywhere else."

African-American leader Frederick Douglass, on a visit to Dublin before the start of the Potato Famine, described the people and their horrible living conditions:

> The spectacle that affected me most, and made the most vivid impression on my mind . . . was the frequency with which I met little children in the street at a late hour of the night, covered with filthy rags, and seated upon cold stone steps, or in corners, leaning against brick walls, fast asleep, with none to look upon them, none to care for them. . . . During my stay in Dublin, I took occasion to visit the huts of the poor in its vicinity—and of all places to witness human misery, ignorance, degradation, filth and wretchedness, an Irish hut is pre-eminent. . . . Here you have an Irish hut of cabin, such as millions of the people of Ireland live in. And some live in worse than these. Men and women, married or single, old and young, lie down together, in much the same degradation as the American slaves.

A German traveler to Milwaukee, Wisconsin, in 1854 described the competition between the Irish and Germans in the draying business, based on his experience after arriving by boat: "The Irish want to claim this trade for themselves exclusively, and begrudge the Germans their small earnings. When, despite the importunities, we hired the only German cart that had come out from town, the Irish followed us a good distance with abuses and insults against the 'Dutchman' and finally even with stones. Our German carter was rather fearful and timid in the face of these insolent Irish."

Bernhard Domschke described the reluctance of German immigrants to join the Irish as members of the Democratic party in 1854. He later became the chief spokesman for the Milwaukee German Republicans: ". . . In our struggle we are not concerned with nationality, but with principles; we are for liberty, and against union with Irishmen who stand nearer barbarism and brutality than civilization and humanity. The Irish are our natural enemies, not because they are Irishmen, but because they are the truest guards of Popery."

California, and Alaska. Conditions in the mines were terrible, and cave-ins frequently killed workers. Wages paid were typically low, and miners were also forced to give most of their earnings back to the mining company to buy food and equipment and pay rent for company housing.

Families who could not earn enough on only the husband's salary had to rely on supplemental wages to feed and clothe their children. For some, an older, unmarried, or teenage son or daughter found work to earn an additional salary, but usually, every able-bodied family member was sent out to find work. Children even roamed the streets of the Irish neighborhoods, selling newspapers, matches, or apples. "Corn girls" sold ears of sweet corn out of boiling pots, while boys worked shining shoes. Kids with nothing to sell turned to begging and, if that didn't work, outright theft to add to the family income.

In the coal-mining regions of Pennsylvania, young boys went to work with their fathers sorting rock from the lumps of coal. Girls were often hired with their parents in the textile mills and spent hours each day threading machines by hand.

WORK FOR WOMEN

Married women with families to care for had few well-paying options for work. The main occupation for them was to take in boarders. This allowed women to keep their families together, maintain their homes, and raise their children while still earning some income, usually an average of $1.25 each week. Others worked at home sewing or taking in laundry. As many as one-third of women age 30 or younger worked in the needle trades at mid-century, but received notoriously low wages. Those with families left their children under the care of their oldest daughter or were able to work at home and be paid a set rate for each piece of clothing they produced. The *New York Tribune* reported one example in 1853 in which women received only $0.08 for a completed shirt.

To earn enough to sustain the family, Irish-American children frequently found themselves put to work at a young age. Some sold matches, corn, or newspapers in the street, while the more skilled (like these two girls) made lace for a dollar a week.

Most factory and mill workers were single women. These seamstresses, dressmakers, milliners (hat-makers), and lace-makers performed repetitive tasks for long hours in poorly lighted factories for an average of less than $0.50 each week. Other better-paid mill or factory jobs averaged up to $5.50 each week and employed women making umbrellas, boxes, or paper flowers. Other jobs open to women included book printers and binders, and shopkeepers. Women with no other options frequently turned to prostitution.

By far the most popular form of employment for unmarried women was to work as a domestic servant in the homes of the city's wealthy families or in hotels and boarding houses. They were given a uniform to wear and room and board within the household, which reduced the burden on the rest of their family. In addition, they were paid between $4.00 and $8.00 each month, most of which could be put into savings.

Most women had much to learn before they were able to perform their duties. Even simple tasks such as washing windows or dusting were beyond their experience based on their backgrounds in Ireland. The rigid rules governing setting tables and serving meals took months or years of training. Many began by doing laundry, caring for children, cleaning, or working as kitchen assistants. As their knowledge increased, they supervised other maids, became personal attendants to family members, or became cooks. Working as a "domestic," as they were called, became part of the Irish stereotype, and many wealthy families referred to all their female servants as "Bridget," a common Irish name.

MONEY SENT TO IRELAND

The extra income Irish women earned often made it possible for husbands to remain at home rather than have to travel cross-country to find work. Women were also responsible for sending much of their savings back to Ireland to bring other family members to America. One study in 1867 tallied that more than $120 million was sent to Ireland in the 20-year period since 1847. Between 1848 and 1900, Irish North Americans sent an average of $5 million annually to Ireland, with 90 percent of this coming from families in the United States. This would average out to each immigrant sending back $28.43 to their families each year. With any extra savings going back to Ireland, it was impossible for immigrants to get ahead and move out of the city slums, further entrenching the negative stereotype of the "lazy" Irish.

DISCRIMINATION FUELED BY MEXICAN-AMERICAN WAR INVOLVEMENT

The negative public opinion toward the Irish immigrants was displayed in local newspaper articles, which denounced the Irish for their detrimental impact on American society. Blamed for diseases, unemployment, low wages, and high rates of crime, the Irish could do nothing right in the eyes of the Americans. Editorial cartoons portrayed the Irish as violent alcoholics, with ape-like features. Their lack of education was given as the reason they remained crowded together in the decaying slums. Americans also took offense at the immigrants' nostalgia for their homes and family in Ireland and feared that the Irish could never truly become part of American society.

This fear of national disloyalty was fueled by the actions of some Irish immigrants during the Mexican-American War (1846–1848). Approximately 25 percent of the troops recruited to fight for the United States were Irish, and another 25 percent were immigrants from other nations. During the war, between 100 to 150 soldiers, roughly one-third of them Irish, deserted the U.S. Army and went to fight with a Mexican battalion. Led by an Irishman named John Riley, the deserters fought under a green flag decorated with a shamrock, harp, and figure of Saint Patrick.

The group became known as the San Patricios and gained a reputation for their bravery from their involvement in battles at Monterrey, Buena Vista, and Mexico City. The reasons for their desertion are not completely clear, but many historians point to the racism and discriminatory attitudes of the American troops toward the foreign-born soldiers, especially toward the Irish. Others note that the Irish may have felt an affinity for the Mexican people because of their shared Catholic faith. The Mexican government also offered higher pay or land grants for those who deserted, and survived, which would have been tempting to the immigrants who had joined the army to provide a steady income for their families.

Most paid a high price for their desertion. At the war's outcome, 85 of the San Patricios were captured by the victorious U.S. Army, of which 72 were court-martialed (brought to trial) and 50 were executed.

THE KNOW-NOTHINGS AND OTHER ANTI-IMMIGRANT GROUPS

Public complaints against the Irish soon were championed in reactionary political campaigns. One of the most successful, yet secretive, anti-immigration political groups was the American Party, also called the Know-Nothings, which was founded in 1843. Along with the political party, nativist Americans joined corresponding secret societies such as the Order of the Star Spangled Banner or the Sires of '76. Members were told to respond "I don't know," when asked for information about their society's lodges or membership rites. Their political platform became quite well known, as they pushed for laws to keep Catholics and foreigners out of office. The Know-Nothings also promoted delayed citizenship for immigrants, declaring that they should reside in the United States for 21 years, rather than 5 years, before being allowed to vote, since that was the legal voting age for American men.

During the 1840s and 1850s, the Know-Nothings and other anti-immigrant parties such as the Native American Party and American Republican Party had some limited success. By making the Irish the scapegoats of many issues such as rising crime, crowded conditions in cities, and labor problems, the Know-Nothings fostered an "us versus them" mentality to isolate the Irish. Rather than force the public and elected officials to face up to the challenges of a growing population, centering on the Irish as the root of the problem provided a simple solution: "get rid of the Irish." This tactic garnered support in some elections, as the governorship in Massachusetts and the majority in seven state legislatures were won by party members in 1854–55. There were also 90 Know-Nothings elected to the 34th Congress in 1855.

Nativists were also successful in passing restrictive immigration laws in some states. These laws were later struck down by the Supreme Court, who declared that only Congress could make immigration decisions. The Know-Nothings later broke up over the issue of slavery, which they supported, and most anti-immigration feelings cooled as the country became divided before the outbreak of the Civil War.

MOVING TOWARD ASSIMILATION

The national division over the issue of slavery during the Civil War diverted much attention away from immigration issues. Involvement in the war also allowed Irish immigrants to gain a toehold toward assimilation in their new home. The prejudice and discrimination of Americans, based on ideas about the immigrants' poverty, living conditions, and occupations caused the Irish to identify more strongly with one another as a group. Although this slowed their acceptance by mainstream society in many ways, they used their cultural pride and banded together to fight for equal treatment. This led to a distinctive Irish influence on many aspects of American life in the late 1800s. This extended well into the twentieth century, including politics, the labor movement, religion, and education.

CHAPTER

6 AFTER THE FAMINE

As the Famine immigrants found niches in the American workforce and settled into the existing Irish communities, they began to focus on adapting to the new world around them. The initial prejudice they faced actually had a positive effect on the formation of a unique Irish-American culture in America. By retaining aspects of their Irish heritage, they were able to influence and reshape parts of American society that have been strongly associated with the Irish at different times in America's history. The Democratic political party received much early grass-roots support, and later leadership, from Irish voters. Much of the driving force behind the formation of unions in the labor movement of the late 1800s came from the suffering of the Irish workman as he built the great industries of America. The Irish transplanted and expanded upon the traditions of their Catholic faith and strengthened the American Catholic Church. One such example of this expansion and strengthening was the development of the parochial school system in the United States. All these arenas provided Irish immigrants with the chance to

When the Civil War erupted, the Irish proved themselves capable soldiers, most fighting for the Union Army. In all, the Union boasted 38 Irish regiments, the most famous being Colonel Matthew Murphy's "Fighting 69th."

pursue the American dream, but also gave them the chance to be a part of American culture, rather than an immigrant group pushed to the fringe of society.

IRISH MEN IN THE CIVIL WAR

The Famine immigrants became involved in shaping American history at the outbreak of the Civil War (1861–1865). Irish men, like their native-born American neighbors, enlisted in both the Union and Confederate armies. The motivations for Irish enlistment were varied. Some saw military life as an opportunity for a salary to provide for their family. Others, who had often enlisted in local state militia groups on arrival in America, saw the war as an opportunity to gain military experience, which they someday hoped to use back in Ireland to oust the British. Many in the North feared that the abolition of slavery would lead to fierce competition for jobs; so they fought to protect their own financial interests. Undoubtedly, many were grateful for the chance at a new life that emigration had provided and sought to defend their new home and families.

Still other Irish were forced by circumstances to become involved in the war. In 1863, Congress passed the first draft law in history, which required all able-bodied men ages 20 to 45 to enlist for a three-year term. Men could avoid enlisting if they could find a substitute to take their place or pay $300—roughly equal to the annual wage of a laborer—to waive the requirement. Some Irish workingmen resented this exemption as a clause that favored the wealthy and sent far more lower-class men into action. Their anger was turned against the group they held responsible for the Civil War, the African Americans. Up to 200,000 Irish formed mobs who attacked 10,000 black residents, injuring or killing 1,200 people in New York City's Draft Riots and burned down the Colored Orphan Asylum. Federal troops were called in to restore order after four days of riots in the city. The Irish were condemned as savage animals in the eyes of the public, and discrimination against the immigrants became more deeply ingrained.

Even with this strike against them, as a group the Irish became known in both the Confederacy and Union for their valor (bravery) in battle. Five Irish-born generals fought in the South, with Irish units raised in Alabama, Georgia, Missouri, North and South Carolina, Texas, Tennessee, and Virginia. Most Louisiana regiments had a majority of Irish enlisted men, and New Orleans produced its own Irish Brigade. The North had an even more notable Irish presence. There were 38 Irish regiments in the Union Army, the most famous being New York's "Fighting 69th," which was later incorporated into the "Irish Brigade" now memorialized at Antietam National Battlefield. Nearly 150,000 Irish-born men fought in the Union Army, and hundreds of thousands of second-generation Irish filled the ranks of both the North and the South. Americans saw that the Irish were willing to fight and die to defend the nation. This ended a great deal of the hostility toward the Irish and dispelled the idea that they were disloyal to America.

ANOTHER WAVE OF IRISH IMMIGRATION

Even with their war involvement providing the first steps toward acceptance in America, the Irish still faced discrimination, particularly based on their Catholicism. Emerging political groups such as the American Protective Association held anti-Catholic and anti-immigration views, and some even felt that the only solution was to send Irish immigrants back to Ireland. This became especially true as another era of emigration began in the late 1870s.

In Ireland, the people who had survived the Famine still faced continuing poverty and joblessness. Farm labor, which rebounded with healthy potato crops, was affected in the late 1800s by the increasing use of farm equipment such as harvesters and cultivators, reducing the need for human laborers. There were also additional crop failures and dropping prices in the 1870s and 1880s, resulting in another wave of tenant evictions by landlords. Industry had not been developed in Ireland, so cities held few jobs. From the end of the Famine in 1855 until 1921, when Ireland became independent from Britain, more than 3 million immigrants arrived in America. Many of these men and women traveled with tickets paid for by family members already in the United States. By 1890, there were 4.8 million first- and second-generation Irish in the United States and just under 5 million in 1900, when the population of Ireland was only 4.5 million.

Unlike the earlier Famine families who emigrated together, these later immigrants were usually young and single. Frequently, it was the oldest son or daughter who made the journey alone, then sent for other siblings one by one, until the entire family could be reunited in America. The Irish were unique among late-nineteenth-century immigration groups in that there were as many women emigrating as men, and in some years, more. Job prospects for them in Ireland were dismal. Marriage was often delayed, since families could not provide dowries for their daughters because of financial hardship. Potential grooms who could provide for a wife and family became more scarce. This was because partible inheritance of land ended, meaning that only one son could now receive property, and therefore landless young men immigrated to America. So more and more single young women immigrated. The extra income earned by single and married Irish women in America provided most of the funding that was sent back to Ireland's impoverished families.

GUILT AT LEAVING IRELAND

Even with the financial reasons for emigration before them, the decision to leave the family often created an emotional dilemma for emigrants. Irish family members had a strong sense of loyalty to one another, as well as a loyalty to their community and country. Children were raised to be obedient to their parents, and dutiful children would stay close and support their elders through difficult times. Emigration forced a choice between keeping the family together and leaving home to financially support the rest of the family. Emigrants felt guilt at "abandoning" their family in time of need, even though it was essential in order to save them.

NEW IRISH-AMERICAN CULTURE

These new immigrants, arriving in America after the Famine in 1855 and into the early 1900s, initially faced much of the same discrimination as the Famine immigrants, which caused them to group together even more closely. As the Irish became settled in America, they transplanted aspects of their native culture to make their new home more familiar and comfortable. This was the formation of a new Irish-American culture. As in Ireland, neighbors relied on each other for emotional and sometimes financial support. Entire families would attend weddings, christenings, or wakes, where Irish music and customs reminded them of home. Dances, fairs, or Saint Patrick's Day festivals often provided an opportunity for young people to meet. Young men frequented bars in their free time, or they might attend sporting events such as dogfights or boxing matches. Many would take their girlfriends to plays or dances that featured Irish reels and jigs. Young men also joined local militia groups or political clubs.

YOUNG WOMEN IMMIGRANTS

Young women may have found themselves having free time for the first time in their lives. Working as a domestic servant in a rich family's home allowed single Irish women to gain a great deal of personal independence and freedom. In Ireland, most would have faced a life of grubbing potatoes for their parents until they married and grubbed potatoes for their husbands. In America, they had their own income, room and board, and few personal expenses. They even received one day off each week—unheard of for farm laborers in the old country.

Because of this newfound economic independence, many young Irish women in America waited to marry until their 30s or 40s, years later than they would have in Ireland. They usually married Irish men, often people they had known in Ireland before they had emigrated or who were natives of their home counties and shared a similar background. Most raised an average of three to four children. They faced the possibility of early widowhood, however, because of the frequent casualties of men who suffered from industrial accidents in railroad, mining, or construction jobs. This often left families with no steady or adequate source of income, which often forced children to enter the workforce at an early age. Census records from the late 1800s show many heads of households as women, who had to rely on public assistance or friends and relatives to survive.

SUPPORT ORGANIZATIONS

Immigrants also turned to organizations with ties to their home country for help. Irish societies continued to provide financial assistance to poverty-stricken immigrants and sponsored social events to preserve Irish traditions as well. New York's Irish Emigrant Society tried to counsel new arrivals to help them avoid the alcoholism, theft, and violence of the Irish slum areas. Some of these agencies served all Irish immigrants, whereas others, like the Sligo Young Men's Association, attracted members from a specific area of Ireland. But more and more, Irish immigrants turned to their Catholic faith for support. Local priests served as advisers in communities, and the church provided a refuge where the Irish immigrants felt truly accepted within American society.

Another aspect that further distinguished the Irish immigrants from the American society around them was their strong emotional tie to Ireland and their opposition to what they felt was continued British domination of their native country. Their strong sentiments regarding Irish nationalism were based on the fact that they felt they had been forced to leave Ireland against their wishes, and most still had family and friends there. Irish-American newspapers in America such as the *Irish World*, *Irish Citizen*, and the *Irish News* promoted the notion of the exploitation of Ireland by Britain. Many Irish felt that immigrating to the United States had provided them with a place of refuge, where they could regroup and gain strength before returning to Ireland to work toward national independence.

IRISH-AMERICAN MILITANT GROUPS FOCUS ON IRELAND

In the late 1860s, many Irish immigrants joined the Fenian Brotherhood, a society dedicated to removing British control from Ireland. The group was founded in New York City in 1858 by John O'Mahoney, an exiled leader of an Irish rebellion that took place in 1848. By 1865, there were 250,000 members of the group donating money and support to the cause. Many of the supporters were Civil War veterans and state militia members who hoped to use their American military experience in the armed services to free Ireland.

Some of the militant Fenians attempted to promote their cause by drawing attention to British control of Canada. In 1866, and again in 1870, the Fenian Irish Republican Army, including thousands of Civil War veterans, invaded Canada to try to hold the nation as ransom. They planned to retreat from Canada only when the British agreed to free Ireland. Neither invasion proved successful and again fostered the notion that the Irish were not loyal members of American society. The Irish felt that there was no contradiction in their efforts toward Ireland's freedom, since the founding fathers of America had gone through the same struggle in trying to overthrow British control nearly a century earlier.

Many Irish Americans retained strong ties to their homeland, some forming nationalist groups that raised funds and arms to oppose British rule of Ireland. One group unsuccessfully attempted to hold Canada hostage until the British released their hold on Ireland, while another, led by Charles Stewart Parnell (seen here), sought improved living conditions for Ireland's poor.

Another militant nationalist group called Clan na Gael became influential during the 1880s. This secret society, headed by Irish-born John Devoy, raised funds that were used in Ireland to help make the 1916 Easter Rebellion possible. Another approach for improved conditions in Ireland that had support in America was promoted by Charles Stewart Parnell, who favored Home Rule. This would include the reestablishment of an Irish Parliament that would function within the political framework of British control. A more radical proposal was Michael Davitt's notion of the nationalization of land in Ireland. He believed that private property ownership should be abolished and that the state should control the land, making it equally available as rental property to all tenant farmers. He formed an American Land League, tied to the Irish Land League organization, and his sister Fanny formed the Ladies' Land League in 1880.

Although Devoy, Parnell, and Davitt worked together in a loose alliance called the New Departure to try to reach their different aims—and were successful in raising hundreds of thousands of dollars for famine relief and support of nationalist groups in Ireland—Davitt's ideal of national property control was too liberal for Parnell and Devoy. The partnership split into their separate focus groups again. Nationalism continued to be a focal point of the Irish-American identity until the Irish Free State was formed in 1921, separating the Catholic southern portion of Ireland from the Protestant North.

CONTINUING STRUGGLES AGAINST DISCRIMINATION AND POVERTY

It was evident to the Irish that the discrimination and poverty they had found in the United States when they settled was not going to quickly change. Many of the customs they adopted as coping mechanisms, often through no choice of their own, provided fuel to the argument of many Americans that the Irish were too different to ever assimilate. Living in all-Irish communities, accepting low-paying and high-risk jobs, marrying within the Irish population, and following their separate religious and social traditions further set the Irish apart. They soon adapted many aspects of their Irish subculture, such as Catholicism, loyalty within their community, and even settlement patterns, to meet their changing needs and achieve a measure of success in America.

GROWTH OF CATHOLIC POPULATION

In post-Famine Ireland, many struggled to find work in the depressed economy. Some unmarried young men and women turned to the Catholic Church and became priests and nuns. Many of them also immigrated to America to provide leadership and counsel to the immigrant community. Their numbers swelled the ranks of the clergy; by 1900, more than half of all Catholic priests and nuns in the United States were of Irish descent. Membership in the church grew rapidly during this period as well. Between 1850 and 1900, the number of U.S. Catholics swelled from 1.5 million to more than 12 million members, making the Catholic Church the largest Christian denomination in America. In 1875, John McCloskey became the first Irish-American cardinal in the church, but by 1900, 75 percent of all cardinals and bishops were Irish.

Catholic priests and nuns not only served the immigrants' religious needs, but also provided a great deal of public assistance to meet the unique needs of their immigrant parishioners. The church became the center of the immigrant community, and the parish priest became a highly respected individual. He was relied on to advise and guide church members in matters ranging from disciplining children, to alcoholism, unemployment, and bereavement. The church also sponsored athletic clubs, temperance organizations, and social groups within the community. Sermons were also used to promote certain political parties or candidates who could be helpful to the Irish community.

Parishioners showed their devotion to their faith by donating any change that could be spared for the collection plates at weekly services. Additional churches and cathedrals, seminaries and convents, hospitals, orphanages, homes for the elderly, soup kitchens, and schools were built with these offerings and were staffed by dedicated nuns. In this way, the entire community felt they had played a part in constructing these buildings and could take pride in the lasting, and publicly visible, accomplishments of their ethnic group. These financial donations did slow the movement of immigrants into the middle class, however.

BIRTH OF CATHOLIC EDUCATION

One of the main focuses of the Irish community as they began to emerge from their extreme poverty was the education of their children. Public schools were available for them to attend in many urban areas, but these were run according to a heavily Protestant curriculum, including Bible teachings that criticized the Catholic faith. Irish Catholics felt it was absolutely necessary to educate their children without eroding their religious beliefs and embarked on an ambitious building project to construct a school within each parish community. The goal was to educate children in a disciplined, orderly system while promoting and developing their faith against the criticism of the surrounding Protestant culture. Because funds could not be raised quickly by the poor immigrant community, Irish leaders made requests for public funding of parochial schools. This caused an outcry from the Protestant community, who refused to allow their tax money to fund Catholic education programs, and this funding was denied. By 1900, only 37 percent of Catholic communities had their own private schools.

Colleges and universities were also built in the late 1800s, starting with Georgetown University in Washington, D.C.,

Many Irish immigrants supported a strong Catholic education for their children. Some helped found schools like this one in New York to ensure that their religious traditions would be passed to the next generation.

in 1879. Loyola University in Chicago, Boston College, Marquette University in Wisconsin, and Villanova University in Philadelphia all were founded during the mid-1800s. The University of Notre Dame, though founded in Indiana by French priests in 1842, soon became associated with the Irish. A large percentage of the teachers at these institutions were also of Irish descent.

IRISH INFLUENCE ON POLITICS

It was the sheer number of immigrants, one of the main complaints of the Americans around them, which the Irish turned into an advantage. This was done on election day as the Irish became a force in American politics in the late 1860s. Earlier arrivals had often experienced exploitation by politicians. Representatives of local election hopefuls met incoming immigrant ships at the docks and escorted the passengers to the polls to vote for his candidate, promising jobs and other favors along the way. Over time, the Irish habitually voted as a bloc for a particular candidate. Politicians soon discovered that the ethnic loyalty of the Irish extended to those who could help them. They secured votes by promising jobs and other financial assistance to the Irish communities.

Some historians claim the Irish were fooled into voting "early and often" because of their lack of education, poor understanding of the issues, and financial desperation, but there is a question as to which group was taking advantage of the other—the politicians or the Irish. As Irish groups continued to vote together, their community often received benefits, and individual voters were often rewarded with more "respectable" jobs within the administration's power, such as firefighters, police officers, or construction contractors for local projects.

The Irish recognized that through political control they could challenge the group in power that was the source of prejudice against them. Although they initially "voted in" candidates sympathetic to their situation, the Irish bloc captains or ward captains who canvassed (solicited or asked for) the community for votes gained experience as political organizers. Over time, the Irish promoted and voted for their own candidates in local and state elections. Of course, their ability to enter politics was made easier for them than for other immigrant groups because they spoke English.

Although there was some anti-Catholic reaction to their political involvement, Americans soon recognized that they could no longer think of or dismiss the Irish as a fringe group. In cities such as Boston, Chicago, and New York, Irish voters were a majority in some precincts, where they elected Irish candidates in the late 1800s.

The Kennedy Family

Rose Elizabeth Fitzgerald and Joseph Patrick Kennedy, both grandchildren of Potato Famine emigrants, wed in 1914. During Franklin Roosevelt's presidency, Kennedy served as head of the Securities and Exchange Commission and the Maritime Commission and was named Ambassador to England in 1938. He resigned this post in 1940 after making controversial statements that appeared to favor Adolf Hitler. His own political ambitions dashed, he turned to furthering the careers of his sons before his death in 1969. Rose, who died at the age of 104 in 1995, was also a tireless family campaigner.

Their son John Fitzgerald Kennedy was elected as the first Irish Catholic president of the United States. While president, JFK raised awareness of civil rights issues and established the Peace Corps before being assassinated in 1963. As First Lady, his wife Jacqueline Bouvier Kennedy established the White House Historical Association. She was involved in many charities before her death from cancer in 1994.

John's younger brother, Robert Francis Kennedy, served as U.S. Attorney General during JFK's administration, and was elected U.S. Senator of New York in 1964. He was killed while campaigning for the Democratic presidential nomination for in 1968. Robert's widow, Ethel, gave birth to their eleventh child six months after his death.

Edward Moore Kennedy, the youngest of the family, has served as U.S. Senator of Massachusetts since 1962. Sister Eunice Kennedy Shriver formed the Special Olympics with her husband, Sargent Shriver, in 1968. Their youngest sister, Jean Kennedy Smith, has been involved with family charities since 1964. President Clinton chose her to be the U.S. Ambassador to Ireland in 1993.

John F. Kennedy's daughter, Caroline Kennedy Schlossberg, is a patron of the arts. Her brother, John F. Kennedy, Jr., was killed in a plane crash with

New York State saw some of the earliest and most influential Irish political activity. The state Democratic Party headquarters, known as Tammany Hall, used and cultivated Irish support for its candidates, mainly because it was one party that had not developed a "nativist" ideology. Non-Irish candidates such as Mike Walsh in the 1840s and William Marcy "Boss" Tweed in

his wife and sister-in-law in 1999. He had been involved in numerous charities including the Special Olympics.

The Shriver children are closely involved in their parent's Special Olympics organization, with Timothy serving as director and Robert as a fundraiser. Anthony has been an activist for the mentally disabled. Mark has turned to politics and was elected as a Maryland state legislator in 1994. Maria reports on politics as a news correspondent for NBC.

Patricia Kennedy Lawford and her children maintain a private life. Her daughter Robin has been a fundraiser for the Kennedy Child Study Center, a school for the developmentally disabled.

Robert Kennedy's eldest, Kathleen Kennedy, was elected Lieutenant Governor of Maryland in 1994 and 1998. Her brother, Joseph Patrick Kennedy II, was elected as a U.S. Representative from Massachusetts in 1986. Mary Courtney Kennedy and Mary Kerry Kennedy both work as a human-rights activists.

Jean Kennedy Smith's son, William Smith, is the Director of the Center for International Rehabilitation and founder and president of the organization Physicians Against Land Mines.

Edward Kennedy's children, Edward Jr. and Kara, have been heavily involved with organizations for the disabled. Youngest son Patrick Joseph was elected as the U.S. Representative from Rhode Island in 1994 and was the Assistant Secretary of State during the Clinton administration.

The Kennedys have suffered from tragedies surrounding the untimely deaths of their loved ones, which the American public also mourned. Although some Kennedys have been involved in personal scandals and charges of corruption, the Kennedy traditions of political and charitable involvement continue to shape America.

the late 1850s were elected to party leadership with the help of Irish voters. Tweed was later replaced by the first Irish leader, "Honest John" Kelly, who was elected to power from 1872 to 1886, when the corrupt Tweed was jailed because of a scandal over preferred hiring practices in public construction projects. Irish control of the Democratic Party in New York lasted until the 1940s.

The Irish followed a leadership system of demand and supply: determine what your constituency (citizen in a certain district) needs, use political offices and power to meet those needs, and thereby ensure reelection. Irish administrations did not avoid accusations of corruption, as voters were paid to cast ballots, votes cast for the opposition were destroyed in elections, or the police force kept opposition voters away from the polls. The candidates tried to show their dedication to their constituency by providing jobs, attending funerals, giving financial assistance to the bereaved families, or feeding those who were poor or whose apartments had burned. At a time when the resources of local church and private aid organizations had been exhausted by the vast numbers of people seeking help, this political assistance was crucial. And there was no organized system of government aid for health, employment, or legal services for impoverished immigrants. Tammany's system became the pattern for other major political party organizations.

IRISH AMERICANS IN POLITICAL OFFICES

Boston also had a considerable Irish political presence. In 1886, the first Irish mayor, Hugh O'Brien, was elected and was followed by other Irish leaders including John F. "Honey Fitz" Fitzgerald, maternal grandfather of John F. Kennedy. Kennedy's paternal grandfather Patrick J. Kennedy, also born in Boston, was a member of both the Massachusetts House of Representatives and Senate. In Chicago, Irish influence appeared at nearly the turn of the century, with Michael "Hinky Dink" Kenna and

"Bathhouse John" Coughlin holding power from 1895 into the 1930s. Irish support helped to elect Anton Cermak in 1931 as mayor, and he was followed by 50 years of Irish-American mayors, including Richard J. Daley, who served for 21 years before his death in 1976. Most Irish political power has been held at a local level, although the first Irish-American Catholic nominee for president was Charles O'Connor from New York in 1872. In 1928, Irish-American Alfred E. Smith was nominated and was also defeated. His defeat has been attributed to his Catholic faith. It was not until the election of John F. Kennedy in 1960 that a Catholic was elected president. Many other presidents had been of Irish ancestry, but Kennedy was the first Catholic. Even during his campaign, Kennedy's religion was a matter of concern to many voters.

IRISH-AMERICAN INFLUENCE ON LABOR CONDITIONS

The Irish used the experience of banding together as a group for social and economic benefits not only in politics, but to influence the labor situation in the late 1800s as well. Wealthy industry leaders were making a fortune at the expense of their laborers, but few Americans felt that there should be any kind of labor regulations. They felt this would slow the advances of American businesses that were closing the distance between the United States and economic world leaders such as England and Germany. Famine immigrants first used group protests and strikes to try to acquire better wages and safer working conditions in canal and construction projects in the 1840s and 1850s. Most laborers worked 10 to 12 hours each day of a six-day week in dangerous or unhealthy conditions.

A secret society of mine workers called the Molly Maguires emerged in the anthracite coal region of Pennsylvania in the early 1860s. They combined strike methods with armed destruction of company property to emphasize their demands. Members dynamited mines, and nine foremen were killed in the

In the 1860s, a secret society of Irish miners called the Molly Maguires attempted to improve the working conditions of miners through acts of violence. Although the Molly Maguires dynamited mines and killed foremen, conditions in the mines remained unchanged, and 20 members of the secret society were hanged in Pottsville, Pennsylvania.

violence. Mine owners hired detective James McParlan to infiltrate the group, and he later turned in the leaders to the police. Fifty Irish members were tried for murder, 20 were hanged, and the rest imprisoned. The group disbanded with no improvements made at the mine. The truth surrounding the entire incident is somewhat questionable, since the only surviving accounts of the society's actions are those of the groups that opposed it. However, the secret organizing and vengeful destruction of property bring to mind the actions of desperate tenant farmers in Famine Ireland. Even so, the executed Molly Maguires were granted posthumous pardons more than 100 years later.

LABOR UNIONS

The varied occupations of Irish immigrants in the late 1800s are reflected in the sometimes elaborate names of labor unions. The American Miners Association, the Shoemakers Union, the

Longshoremen's and Laborers' United Benevolent Society, and the International Labor Union became widespread in the 1860s and 1870s and favored group solidarity in strikes and boycotts over violent actions to get results. Irish Americans were often the largest ethnic group within these unions, and many quickly took leadership roles. P. J. McGuire organized the Brotherhood of Carpenters and Joiners, was a founder of the American Federation of Labor in 1886, and is known as "the Father of Labor Day," which Congress established in 1894. The Knights of Labor emerged from the Shoemaker's Union, The Knights of St. Crispin, to become a nationwide society of 750,000 members in the 1880s. They were led by Irish-American Terence Powderly, who had been born in the anthracite region of Pennsylvania. The Knights of St. Crispin included both male and female members. Women such as Kate Mullaney, who organized laundresses, and Leonora O'Reilly, who worked with the United Garment Workers of America and helped start the Women's Trade Union League, were members. Irish-American Mary Kenney O'Sullivan became the first woman organizer of the American Federation of Labor in 1892. By 1900, Irish Americans were the presidents of more than 50 of the 110 member unions within the American Federation of Labor.

Over time, gradual improvements were made within industries, and Irish-American leadership in unions has continued into the twentieth century, marked by George Meany becoming the first head of the nation's largest union, the combined AFL-CIO (American Federation of Labor and Congress of Industrial Organizations) in 1955.

GAINING ACCEPTANCE AND MOVING UP

The Irish gained increasing acceptance by Americans during the last few decades of the 1800s. The second- and even third-generation Irish seemed less "foreign" than the many groups of southern and eastern Europeans who flooded into America in the 1890s. The Irish spoke English and had Anglo-Saxon features, which made them seem more American. Many of the stereotypical ideas about the Famine Irish were dispelled by the arrival of the later immigrants, who were not destitute, had better educations and strong family ties. The influx of all new immigrant groups also made American society less ethnically homogeneous in nature and reduced some of the opposition to the Irish simply for the reason that they were different. Although anti-immigration laws were still being passed into the 1880s and 1890s, many of them focused on "undesirable" individuals such as criminals or those with mental disabilities rather than one nationality in particular.

By the 1900s, Irish-Americans had begun to infiltrate the American middle class. Political control directly influenced the economic situation of Irish families across the country, and the labor movement had improved the working conditions for countless traditionally "Irish" occupations. Although they were separated from the mainstream culture, the immigrants' children earned their educations at the newly constructed parochial schools and Catholic universities and were able to pursue more middle- and upper-class careers as teachers, lawyers, doctors, or nurses. As the immigrants' economic situation improved, they were able to leave the slum tenements to purchase homes of their own in middle-class neighborhoods, fulfilling a dream for native-born Irish who had been forbidden to buy property in Ireland.

In addition, the church and all its educational and charitable organizations became a source of pride for Irish Americans for generations. Catholic teachings promoted values that were similar to those of the mainstream American culture. Temperance, hard work, and devotion to family were some of their ideals, making it easier for the immigrants to assimilate. Even with these political, economic, and social accomplishments, many Irish families did not escape the lower-class "shanty Irish" designation to enter the ranks of the middle-class "lace curtain Irish" until after World War II.

Perhaps the factor that most helped Irish immigrants become part of American society was their actual presence in all parts of the country. Even though more than half of the over 4 million Irish immigrants settled in New York, Philadelphia, Boston, and Chicago in a settlement tradition that continued until 1920, all parts of America had Irish communities. Southern states such as Kentucky and the Carolinas saw Scotch-Irish pioneers such as Daniel Boone and Davey Crockett in the late 1700s and early 1800s, whereas port cities became home for thousands of Famine immigrants mid-century. Canal and railroad jobs brought Irish workers to the Midwest, where they became involved in industry and to some extent, agriculture. Irish muscle helped to rebuild Chicago after the devastating fire of 1871. In the West, Irish became trappers, miners, and loggers.

Butte, Montana, home of the Anaconda copper mine run by Irish-born Marcus Daly, held the title of the most Irish town in the United States in the 1880s. The West and Southwest saw Irish cowboys, ranchers, and "Indian fighters" in the years after the Civil War. Miners traveled as far as the gold fields of Alaska, bringing an Irish element halfway around the world from its homeland. By spreading to all parts of the United States, Irish Americans could no longer be considered a group of outsiders. Their increasing presence led to their full acceptance in America during the 1900s.

CHAPTER

7 INTO THE MELTING POT: The Irish-American Influence

There are currently more than 38 million Americans, one out of every seven people, who can claim to have Irish ancestry. The Irish in America are no longer marginalized, living in crowded slums, or finding employment at predominantly unskilled jobs. The descendants of those who left Ireland have moved to all parts of the country and live at all socioeconomic levels. They have transformed themselves from being targets of anti-immigration laws to becoming the lawmakers themselves, as senators, representatives, and presidents of the United States. Presidents with Irish ancestors include Andrew Jackson, Woodrow Wilson, John F. Kennedy, Richard Nixon, Ronald Reagan, and William Jefferson Clinton.

So much have the Irish become part of America that their traditions and concerns are shared by many others whose

Irish culture is no longer limited to small-scale celebrations in all-Irish communities. People of all ethnic backgrounds celebrate St. Patrick's Day on March 17 of every year, a day when "Everyone's Irish."

names are not Patrick and Bridget. St. Patrick's Day parades are held in cities across the nation, and those who cannot attend them can wear green, eat corned beef and cabbage, and watch the New York parade on television. Catholicism, rather than being a religion to be feared, is shared by individuals from numerous other ethnic groups, including French, German, Hispanic, and Italian Americans. The parochial schools founded for Irish immigrant children now welcome students from all ethnic backgrounds. And the nationalism and concern over the "Irish troubles" has become an international issue, as the Belfast ("Good Friday") Agreement brokered by U.S. President Bill Clinton in 1998 brought the struggle between Irish republicans and Northern Ireland separatists to a tenuous truce.

A new wave of Irish emigration occurred during the 1980s, when high unemployment levels in Ireland caused thousands of legal and illegal immigrants to leave their homes. Many of the legal immigrants were highly educated professionals who sought job opportunities in Britain, Europe, and the United States. The illegal immigrants were predominantly young, middle-class men and women who entered the United States on tourist visas, but did not leave when their visas expired. They had been unable to acquire legal visas because of U.S. restrictions on the number of visas allotted to each country. But once in the country they found jobs and settled in "new Irish" communities in cities such as New York, Boston, Chicago, or San Francisco. Perhaps as many as 100,000 Irish emigrants entered the United States during the 1980s. In the 1990s, however, the economy of Ireland rebounded, finding new life in computer and software production. These high-tech businesses created thousands of new jobs, and many of the educated Irish who had fled in the 1980s returned to Ireland once the economy was stable.

During the 1980s and 1990s, America has seen a new level of interest in Irish and Irish-American culture. As "cultural pluralism" became a catch phrase during these decades, many Americans became interested in tracing their ethnic heritage and began to pursue newfound traditions of their ancestors. Numerous colleges and universities began offering

Irish Studies coursework and exchange programs. Today, an Irish influence can be seen in many aspects of American popular culture, and this influence can sometimes be traced back for decades.

IRISH AMERICANS IN THE ARTS

One of the earliest areas in which Irish Americans became a part of America was in entertainment. Composers and playwrights such as George M. Cohan and Eugene O'Neill, sons of Irish immigrants, had their stories of Irish families produced on Broadway during the early 1900s. Irish-American producers and directors also became famous for their work. Walt Disney had Irish roots, and John Ford, who was perhaps best known for his Westerns starring John Wayne or for *The Grapes of Wrath*, directed a number of films set in Ireland. The list of Irish-American actors and actresses is long. For example, stars such as James Cagney, Helen Hayes, Gene Kelly, Grace Kelly, Jackie Gleason, Jason Robards, and Carroll O'Connor all share an Irish ancestry. More recent actors and actresses are not even recognized as being Irish American, such as Mia Farrow, Anjelica Huston, Jack Nicholson, Robert Redford, and Brooke Shields. Hollywood has turned to Irish history as a topic in films such as *In the Name of the Father* and *Michael Collins.*

Literature has certainly been influenced by Irish-American authors. Early twentieth-century Irish names such as F. Scott Fitzgerald (*The Great Gatsby*), John O'Hara (*Butterfield 8*), and James T. Farrell (the *Studs Lonigan* trilogy) are often found on today's reading lists. Among recent popular literature, Frank McCourt's *Angela's Ashes* and *'Tis* and Thomas Cahill's *How the Irish Saved Civilization* both saw extended runs on the *New York Times* best-seller list.

The Irish musical tradition can be seen in many areas of American music. The 2002 Grammy Awards evidenced the broad, popular success of this Irish influence. Irish folk

Today, many aspects of Irish culture are celebrated in America. Traditional Irish music and dance have seen a recent resurgence in popularity among American audiences.

music directly influenced the creation of the Appalachian bluegrass genre, finding new exposure via the soundtrack from *Brother, Where Art Thou?*, which earned multiple awards including Album of the Year. Rock music once again bowed to the Irish as U2 earned the Rock Album of the Year with *All That You Can't Leave Behind* nearly two decades after the group's first album debuted. This follows a few years after the music from *Riverdance* won a Grammy, and the performance of traditional Irish jigs and reels in

Notable Irish Americans

Mary Harris "Mother" Jones (c. 1830–1930) Prominent U.S. labor activist, Mother Jones was born in Cork, Ireland and spent most of her life working on behalf of poor workers, and was frequently jailed for her activities. In 1905, she helped to found the Industrial Workers of the World union.

Henry Ford (1863–1947) Born in Dearborn, Michigan, Ford became a self-taught mechanic and left his family's farm at age 16 to become an apprentice in a machine shop. Ford founded the Detroit Automobile Company in 1899 and the Ford Motor Car Company in 1903. Though criticized as an anti-Semite, Ford was also a generous philanthropist. His Ford Foundation, begun in 1936, has issued more than $8 billion in grant money to this day.

Nellie Bly (Elizabeth Cochrane Seaman) (c. 1865–1922) Born in Cochrane Mills, Pennsylvania, Seaman chose the pen name Nellie Bly from a song about a social reformer. As a reporter for the *New York World,* she specialized in exposé stories. In 1889, she was challenged to complete a round-the-world trip faster than that of the fictional Phineas Fogg of Jules Verne's *Around the World in Eighty Days*. She made the trip in 78 days, reporting on her travels as she went.

George M. Cohan (1878–1942) Born in Providence, Rhode Island, on July 3, George Michael Cohan became a famous actor, playwright, director, and composer and was the inventor of the modern musical. He had many hits on Broadway in the early 1900s. The writer of several patriotic songs, including "You're a Grand Old Flag," and "Over There," his life story is the topic of the 1942 movie *Yankee Doodle Dandy*, starring fellow Irish-American, James Cagney.

Eamon De Valera (1882-1975) The New York-born Eamon De Valera was raised by relatives in County Limerick, Ireland. He became involved in the Republican movement and was a commandant in the 1916 Easter Rebellion. Saved from the firing squad by his U.S. citizenship, he continued his involvement in the struggle to remove British control from Ireland. He became the leader for Sinn Féin, the Irish Republicans' political party, from 1917 to 1926. De Valera served as prime minister of Ireland from 1932 to 1948, 1951 to 1954, and again from 1957 to 1959, and president of Ireland from 1959 to 1973.

Georgia O'Keeffe (1887–1986) Born in Sun Prairie, Wisconsin, O'Keeffe contributed to modern art in the United States with her use of color and perspective. She studied painting in Chicago at The Art Institute, New York's Arts Students League, and the Teachers College of Columbia University. The natural, open spaces and light of the desert provided inspiration for O'Keeffe's paintings of skulls and adobe buildings. She wrote a book about her artwork in 1976 and died 10 years later at the age of 98.

Notable Irish Americans *(continued)*

F. Scott Fitzgerald (1896–1940) Born in St. Paul, Minnesota, Francis Scott Key Fitzgerald became instantly famous at the age of 23 for his autobiographical novel *This Side of Paradise*, and is perhaps best remembered for his novel *The Great Gatsby*. Also known for *Tender is the Night*, and the posthumous work *The Last Tycoon*, Fitzgerald published 178 short stories and essays and was a screenwriter during his career. After a personal life marked by difficulties, including heavy debts, alcoholism, and mental breakdowns, Fitzgerald died of a heart attack at age 44.

Tip O'Neill (1912–1994) Born in Cambridge, Massachusetts, Thomas Phillip O'Neill, Jr., ran for office on the City Council while still a student at Boston College. A staunch Democrat, he was elected to the state House of Representatives in 1936, where he served as its youngest speaker from 1947 to 1952. He then became a member of the U.S. House of Representatives, where he served from 1953 to 1987. He was Speaker of the House from 1977 to 1987 and co-wrote his memoirs, *Man of the House: The Life and Political Memoirs of Speaker Tip O'Neill* after his retirement.

Judy Garland (1922–1969) Born Frances Ethel Gumm in Grand Rapids, Minnesota. Garland was a child performer and had taken her stage name by age nine. She appeared in 32 films during her career. She was awarded an Academy Award in 1939 for her performance in *The Wizard of Oz*. Garland's exceptional singing voice was featured in nearly 100 singles and more than a dozen albums. Her recording of "It's a Great Day for the Irish" from the 1940 film *Nellie Kelly* became a favorite of Irish Americans.

Sandra Day O'Connor (1930–) Born in El Paso, Texas, O'Connor spent her first years in southeastern Arizona. She earned her law degree from Stanford University, graduating third in her class in 1952. O'Connor later became the first female justice of the U.S. Supreme Court in 1981. She also served as one of Arizona's state senators from 1969 to 1974, when she left the Senate to become a judge in the Maricopa County Superior Court. She was later appointed to the State Court of Appeals before being named to the Supreme Court by President Ronald Reagan.

synchronized step dances exploded onto American stages.

Irish performers of traditional folk music saw a surge of popularity in the 1960s with the songs of the Clancy Brothers and continue today with groups such as The

Chieftains and Cherish the Ladies. Rock performers such as Van Morrison and Sinéad O'Connor have global popularity, as does the new age artist Enya. The National Public Radio program *The Thistle and Shamrock* features Celtic music of all types each week. Television's Public Broadcasting Service brings The Irish Tenors into our homes. Across the nation, Celtic music festivals attract thousands of fans, who gather to celebrate this musical resurgence. And anyone can visit an Irish pub to enjoy live music, often washed down with a pint of Harp or Guinness.

IRISH AMERICANS IN SPORTS

In sports, Irish-American contributions have been less numerous, but no less successful. The earliest arena to feature Irish immigrants and their offspring was the boxing ring. Bare-knuckle fighting champions from the 1840s through the 1900s included many Irish-born and Irish-Americans, the greatest of whom was John L. Sullivan. He was considered a national hero after his defeat of the Irish heavyweight champion Paddy Ryan in 1882. He became a celebrity, had songs written about him, and was the first to say, "the bigger they are, the harder they fall." He became proud and overweight, and proved his statement correct when he was defeated by fellow Irish-American James "Gentleman Jim" Corbett in 1892. The late 1920s saw Jack Dempsey and Gene Tunney battle together as the last dominant Irish-American boxers in the field.

Baseball was another area of Irish influence. The late 1800s and early 1900s saw so many successful Irish ballplayers that non-Irish hopefuls took Irish names to try to help their careers. John J. McGraw, who was considered by some to be the best manager of all time, was a professional player by the age 16. He managed for three teams, the most successful of which was the New York Giants from

1902 to 1932, when they won 10 National League and three World Championships. McGraw traveled around the world, introducing baseball to Europe and Asia, and was elected to the Baseball Hall of Fame in 1937. Another 1937 inductee was Connie Mack, born Cornelius McGillicuddy, who spent 66 years in the major leagues as a player and manager. His career managing the Philadelphia Athletics (A's) from 1901 to 1950 brought them nine American League and five World Championships. Charles A. Comiskey, son of a Famine immigrant father, played for Milwaukee, helped organize the American League, and owned the Chicago White Sox. The Chicago team now plays in a ballpark bearing Comiskey's name. Noted for being the earliest first baseman to stand away from the base, he was elected into the Hall of Fame in 1939. Irish American Lynn Nolan Ryan pitched for 27 seasons and compiled a record 5,714 strikeouts, 7 no-hitters, and 12 one-hitters during his career. He was inducted into the Hall of Fame in 1999.

Perhaps one of the more visible Irish associations with organized sports comes from team mascots. Boston Celtics basketball and the "Fighting Irish" of the University of Notre Dame both feature leprechauns in team logos. These team names focus on the ethnic heritage of both regions and the character of the Irish in America who strive to persevere against all odds.

★ ★ ★

Irish Americans can be noted as an ethnic group that has successfully and fully assimilated into the United States. Some may say they have done so too well, since Irish Americans can no longer be seen as a distinct group in American culture. They do not face direct discrimination based on their heritage—the "No Irish Need Apply" sentiments of the late 1800s are part of history. Irish-American impact on politics, labor conditions, religion, and American customs can be seen today, and all of us—no matter what our ethnic background—must recognize that much of their history has become American history shared by us all.

400s	The Celts arrive in Ireland.
500–1500	Catholicism spreads throughout Ireland during the Middle Ages.
795	Vikings conquer eastern shore of Ireland.
1014	Brian Boru and his Celtic army ousts Vikings from Ireland.
1155	Normans invade Ireland via England.
1500s	The potato is introduced in Ireland.
1541	England's King Henry VIII declares himself king of Ireland and tries to force Protestantism upon Ireland to establish better political control.
1609	James I brings in settlements of Scottish Protestants to Ulster.
1649	Oliver Cromwell becomes lord protector of England, and begins confiscating large portions of Irish farmland for his supporters, while transporting thousands of Irish to labor in British colonies.
1690	William of Orange defeats Irish army in Battle of the Boyne.
1690s	British laws called Penal Codes are expanded, restricting many Catholic Irish freedoms and rights.
1600s–1770s	Irish immigrate to the British colonies in North America, many agree to work as indentured servants to pay for their passage, others are Protestants leaving Ireland for economic and religious freedom.
1759	First St. Patrick's Day Parade in New York City.
1776	Irish living in the American colonies fight for freedom from English rule during the American Revolution.
1801	The Act of Union between Great Britain and Ireland creates the United Kingdom, and further restricts Irish freedom.
1820s	Population rapidly increases in southern Ireland, forcing larger numbers of Irish Catholics to emigrate to find work.
1820s–1830s	Construction of the Erie and other canal projects employs thousands of Irish workers. Advertisements of these jobs appear in Dublin and Belfast to attract more immigrants.
1834	Anti-Catholic sentiment leads to the destruction of a convent by fire in Massachusetts.
1840s	Nativist political parties such as the Know-Nothings begin to form and influence immigration laws until the late 1800s.
1844	Anti-Catholic riots in Philadelphia destroy churches, and Irish immigrants are injured or killed.

1845	A fungus destroys half the nation's potato crop, starting the Potato Famine. The blight and the period of starvation following it continue until 1855.
1846–1848	Mexican-American War. The desertion of Irish soldiers to join the San Patricios of the Mexican army leads to discrimination against the Irish.
1849	The California Gold Rush attracts numerous Irish immigrants.
1850s–1860s	Railroad construction projects provide jobs and allow for the spread of Irish immigrants throughout the United States.
1855–1921	Largest numbers of Irish immigrants enter the United States for economic reasons after another crop failure in Ireland.
1861–1865	The American Civil War.
1863	Irish mobs in New York City riot in protest of the Civil War draft law.
1866 and 1870	Fenians attempt to invade Canada
1869	The transcontinental railroad is completed at Promontory, Utah.
1872	Charles O'Connor becomes the first Irish Catholic nominated for president of the United States.
1916	Easter Rebellion occurs in Ireland.
1921	Irish Free State is formed, separating Catholic southern Ireland from the Protestant North.
1928	Irish-American Alfred E. Smith loses as the Democratic candidate in the presidential election.
1960	John Fitzgerald Kennedy is elected as the first Catholic president of the United States.
1980s	An economic downturn in Ireland forces a new group of immigrants to enter the United States.

Cahill, Mary Jane. *Northern Ireland.* Philadelphia: Chelsea House, 2000.

Cavan, Seamus. *The Irish-American Experience.* Brookfield, CT: Millbrook Press, 1993.

Clark, Dennis. *Hibernia America: The Irish and Regional Cultures.* New York: Greenwood Press, 1986.

Coffey, Michael, ed., and Terry Golway, text. *The Irish in America.* New York: Hyperion, 1997.

Collier, Christopher, and James Lincoln Collier. *A Century of Immigration: 1820-1924.* Tarrytown, NY: Benchmark Books, 2000.

Conzen, Kathleen. *Immigrant Milwaukee, 1836-1860: Accommodation and Community in a Frontier City.* Cambridge, MA: Harvard University Press, 1976.

Coogan, Tim Pat. *Wherever Green is Worn: The Story of the Irish Diaspora.* New York: Palgrave, 2001.

Coppa, Frank J., and Thomas J. Curran. *The Immigrant Experience in America.* Boston: Twayne Publishers, 1976.

Goodwin, Doris Kearns. *The Fitzgeralds and the Kennedys: An American Saga.* New York: Touchstone, 2001.

Griffin, William D. *The Book of Irish Americans.* New York: Times Books, 1990.

Griffin, William D. *The Irish Americans.* Hong Kong: Hugh Lauter Levin Associates, 1998.

Groneman, Carol. "Working-Class Immigrant Women in Mid-Nineteenth-Century New York: The Irish Woman's Experience." May, 1978. From Pozetta, George E. ed. *Ethnicity and Gender: The Immigrant Woman. American Immigration and Ethnicity.* New York: Garland Publishing, 1991.

Handlin, Oscar. *A Pictoral History of Immigration.* New York: Crown Publishers, 1972.

Hattan, Timothy J. and Jeffrey G. Williamson. *The Age of Mass Migration: Causes and Economic Impact.* New York: Oxford University Press, 1998.

Hoobler, Dorothy and Thomas. *The Irish American Family Album.* Oxford: Oxford University Press, 1995.

Kenny, Kevin. *The American Irish: A History.* New York: Pearson Education, 2000.

Laxton, Edward. *The Famine Ships: The Irish Exodus to America.* New York: Henry Holt & Company, 1996.

Lees, Lynn H. and John Modell. "The Irish Countryman Urbanized: A Comparative Perspective on the Famine Migration." *Journal of Urban History*, vol. 3, no. 4, August 1977. From Pozetta George E, ed. *Emigration and Immigration. American Immigration and Ethnicity*. New York: Garland Publishing, 1991.

MacDonagh, Oliver. "The Irish Famine Emigration to the U.S." From Pozetta George E., ed. *Emigration and Immigration. American Immigration and Ethnicity*. New York: Garland Publishing, 1991.

Mangan, James J., ed. *Robert Whyte's 1847 Famine Ship Diary: The Journey of an Irish Coffin Ship*. Cork, Ireland: Mercier Press, 1994.

Miller, Kerby A. *Paddy's Paradox: Emigration to America in Irish Imagination and Rhetoric*. From Hoerder, Dirk, and Horst Rössler, eds. *Distant Magnets: Expectations and Realities in the Immigrant Experience, 1840-1930*. Ellis Island, NY: Holmes and Meier, 1993.

Moscinski, Sharon. *Tracing Our Irish Roots. American Origins*. Santa Fe, NM: John Muir Publications, 1993.

Murphy, John. *A Little Irish Cookbook* (*Little Cookbook* series). San Francisco: Chronicle Books, 1986.

O'Hara, Megan. *Irish Immigrants, 1840-1920. Coming to America*. Mankato, MN: Blue Earth Books, 2002.

O Muirithe, Diarmaid. *A Seat Behind the Coachman: Travellers in Ireland 1800-1900*. Dublin, Ireland: Gill and MacMillan Ltd., 1972.

Radford, Dwight A. and Kyle J. Betit. *A Genealogist's Guide to Discovering Your Irish Ancestors*. Cincinatti, Ohio: Betterway Books, 2001.

Szucs, Loretto Dennis, and Sandra Hargreaves Luebking. *The Source*. Salt Lake City: Ancestry Incorporated, 1997.

Watts, J. F. *The Irish Americans*. New York: Chelsea House, 1996.

Wells, Ronald A. *Ulster Migration to America: Letters from Three Irish Families*. New York: Peter Lang Publishing, 1991.

Yans-McLaughlin, Virginia, and Marjorie Lightman. *Ellis Island and the Peopling of America: The Official Guide*. New York: The New Press, 1997.

Yetman, Norman R. "The Irish Experience in America." From Orel, Harold, ed. *Irish History and Culture: Aspects of a People's Heritage*. Lawrence, KS: The University Press of Kansas, 1976.

INTERNET RESOURCES

American Antiquarian Society: Canals and Railroads
http://www.americanantiquarian.org/canalsrr.htm

Catholic Encyclopedia: Emigrant Aid Societies
http://www.newadvent.org/cathen/05402b.htm

CIA World Factbook 2002: Ireland
www.odci.gov/cia/publications/factbook/geos/ei.html

The Making of a Melting Pot: Irish Immigration to America from 1700 to the early 1800s (part 1)
http://www.ailf.org/polrep/2001/pr0009.htm

Salon.com: *Who Will Carry the Kennedy Torch?*
http://www.salon.com/news/feature/1999/07/21/torch/index4.html

VIDEO RESOURCES

America, episode 9: *The Huddled Masses.* Producer: BBC/Time-Life Television. Distributed by Ambrose Video Publishing Inc., New York, 1973.

The Irish in America: Long Journey Home. Walt Disney Studios (broadcast on PBS) vol. 1–2.

FICTION

O'Connor, Edwin. *The Last Hurrah.* Boston: Little, Brown, 1956.

NONFICTION

Gallagher, Carol. *The Irish Potato Famine.* Philadelphia: Chelsea House, 2001.

Grenham, John. *Tracing Irish Ancestors: The Complete Guide.* Dublin: Gill and Macmillan, 1999.

Griffen, William D. *The Irish Americans.* Hong Kong: Hugh Lauter Levin Associates, 1998.

Hoobler, Dorothy and Thomas. *The Irish American Family Album.* Oxford: Oxford University Press, 1995.

Kenny, Kevin. *The American Irish: A History.* Studies in Modern History. New York: Pearson Education, 2000.

Laxton, Edward. *The Famine Ships: The Irish Exodus to America.* New York: Henry Holt & Company, 1996.

O'Donnell, Edward T. *1001 Things Everyone Should Know About Irish-American History.* New York: Broadway Books, 2002.

Radford, Dwight A. and Kyle J. Betit. *A Genealogist's Guide to Discovering Your Irish Ancestors: How to Find and Record Your Unique Heritage.* Cincinnati, Ohio: Betterway Books, 2001.

Szucs, Loretto Dennis, and Sandra Hargreaves Leubking, eds. *The Source: A Guidebook of American Genealogy.* Salt Lake City, Utah: Ancestry Incorporated, 1997.

The American Family Immigration History Center at Ellis Island
http://www.ellisisland.org

Family Search
http://www.familysearch.org

The Five Points Site
http://r2.gsa.gov/fivept/fphome.htm

Genealogy.com
http://www.genealogy.com

Grosse Isle and the Irish Memorial
www.parcscanada.gc.ca/parks/quebec/grosseile/en/index.html

Immigration History Research Center at the University of Minnesota
www1.umn.edu/ihrc

The Irish Brigade Memorial at Antietam National Battlefield
http://www.nps.gov/anti/monuments/Irish_B.htm

The Irish In America
http://www.pbs.org/wgbh/pages/irish

Museum of the City of New York
Gaelic Gotham: A History of the Irish in New York
www.mcny.org/irish.htm

The National Archives of Ireland
http://www.nationalarchives.ie

National Archives and Records Administration
http://www.nara.gov

Public Record Office Northern Ireland
http://proni.nics.gov.uk

RootsWeb
http://www.rootsweb.com

USGenWeb Project
http://www.usgenweb.org

Views of the Famine
http://vassun.vassar.edu/~sttaylor/FAMINE

The American Irish Historical Society
991 Fifth Avenue
New York, NY 10028

Embassy of Ireland
2234 Massachusetts Avenue NW
Washington, D.C. 20008

The Irish American Cultural Institute
1 Lackawanna Place
Morristown, NJ 07960

The Irish Arts Center
553 West 51st Street
New York, NY 10019

The Irish Cultural and Heritage Center
2133 W. Wisconsin Avenue
Milwaukee, WI 53223

GENEAOLOGY ORGANIZATIONS

The Family History Library of the Church of Latter-day Saints
35 North West Temple Street
Salt Lake City, UT 84150

Irish Genealogical Society
PO Box 16585
St. Paul, MN 55116-0585

National Genealogical Society
4527 Seventeenth Street North
Arlington, VA 22207-2399

INDEX

CONTRIBUTORS

KERRY GRAVES has been a freelance writer and editor of children's books since 1998. She grew up in Hopkins, Minnesota and earned a BA in English at the University of Minnesota. She later received a degree in secondary education from Central Washington University. She has worked in Madrid, Spain and Washington State as an English and Spanish teacher. Kerry has written many non-fiction books, and is especially interested in American history. Kerry resides in Portland, Oregon with her husband Ritchie, daughter Meagan, and cat Bailey.

DANIEL PATRICK MOYNIHAN is a former United States senator from New York. He is also the only person in American history to have served in the cabinets or subcabinets of four successive presidents—Kennedy, Johnson, Nixon, and Ford. Formerly a professor of government at Harvard University, he has written and edited many books.

PICTURE CREDITS

page:

13: © Adam Woolfitt/Corbis
16: © Corbis
19: © Ted Speigel/Corbis
21: © Kit Kittle/Corbis
23: Hierophant Collection
29: © Sean Sexton Collection/Corbis
32: ©Hulton Archive by Getty Images
37: ©Hulton Archive by Getty Images
43: ©Hulton Archive by Getty Images
46: ©Hulton Archive by Getty Images
50: Associated Press, National Parks Service
53: © Museum of the City of New York/Corbis
56: © Corbis
60: © Bettmann/Corbis
63: © Corbis
67: © Bettmann/Corbis
70: ©Hulton Archive by Getty Images
75: National Archives
81: Collection of the New York Historical Society
88: © Corbis
92: © Bettmann/Corbis
98: © Bettmann/Corbis
103: © Kevin Fleming/Corbis
106: ©Stephanie Maze/Corbis

Cover: © Joseph Sohm; ChromoSohm Inc./CORBIS

Frontis: Courtesy University of Texas at Austin, Perry-Castañeda Map Collection, CIA map.